Steve Martin is a celebrated writer, actor, and performer. His film credits include *The Jerk*, *Father of the Bride* and *Parenthood*, as well as *Roxanne*, *L.A. Story*, and *Bowfinger*, for which he also wrote the screenplays. He has won an Emmy for his television writing and three Grammys. In addition to several plays, including *Picasso at the Lapin Agile* and *Wasp*, he has written collections of comic pieces, *Pure Drivel* and *Cruel Shoes* and the novels *Shopgirl* and *The Pleasure of My Company*. He lives in New York City and Los Angeles.

Also by Steve Martin

NOVELS

The Pleasure of My Company

Shopgirl

PLAYS

Picasso at the Lapin Agile

WASP

NONFICTION

Pure Drivel

Cruel Shoes

SCREENPLAYS

Shopgirl

Bowfinger

L.A. Story

Roxanne

The Jerk (coauthor)

Born

Standing

Up

A Comic's Life

Steve Martin

POCKET
BOOKS

LONDON • SYDNEY • NEW YORK • TORONTO

First published in Great Britain in 2007 by Simon & Schuster UK Ltd
This edition first published by Pocket Books, 2008
An imprint of Simon & Schuster UK Ltd
A CBS COMPANY

1 3 5 7 9 10 8 6 4 2

Simon & Schuster UK Ltd
Africa House
64–78 Kingsway
London WC2B 6AH

www.simonsays.co.uk

Simon & Schuster Australia
Sydney

A CIP catalogue for this book is available
from the British Library

ISBN: 978-1-84739-148-3

Designed by C. Linda Dingler

Text set in Scala

Printed by CPI Cox & Wyman, Reading, Berkshire RG1 8EX

Photograph credits appear on page 209.

To my father, mother,
and sister, Melinda

Contents

Born
Standing
Up

Beforehand

I DID STAND-UP COMEDY for eighteen years. Ten of those years were spent learning, four years were spent refining, and four were spent in wild success. My most persistent memory of stand-up is of my mouth being in the present and my mind being in the future: the mouth speaking the line, the body delivering the gesture, while the mind looks back, observing, analyzing, judging, worrying, and then deciding when and what to say next. Enjoyment while performing was rare—enjoyment would have been an indulgent loss of focus that comedy cannot afford. After the shows, however, I experienced long hours of elation or misery depending on how the show went, because doing comedy alone onstage is the ego's last stand.

1
—

My decade is the seventies, with several years extending on either side. Though my general recall of the period is precise, my memory of specific shows is faint. I stood onstage, blinded by lights, looking into blackness, which made every place the same. Darkness is essential: If light is thrown on the audience, they don't laugh; I might as well have told them to sit still and be quiet. The audience necessarily remained a thing unseen except for a few front rows, where one sourpuss could send me into panic and desperation. The comedian's slang for a successful show is "I murdered them," which I'm sure came about because you finally realize that the audience is capable of murdering you.

Stand-up is seldom performed in ideal circumstances. Comedy's enemy is distraction, and rarely do comedians get a pristine performing environment. I worried about the sound system, ambient noise, hecklers, drunks, lighting, sudden clangs, latecomers, and loud talkers, not to mention the nagging concern "Is this funny?" Yet the seedier the circumstances, the funnier one can be. I suppose these worries keep the mind sharp and the senses active. I can remember instantly retiming a punch line to fit around the crash of a dropped glass of wine, or raising my voice to cover a patron's ill-timed sneeze, seemingly microseconds before the interruption happened.

I was seeking comic originality, and fame fell on me as a by-product. The course was more plodding than heroic: I did not strive valiantly against doubters but took incre-

2
—

mental steps studded with a few intuitive leaps. I was not naturally talented—I didn't sing, dance, or act—though working around that minor detail made me inventive. I was not self-destructive, though I almost destroyed myself. In the end, I turned away from stand-up with a tired swivel of my head and never looked back, until now. A few years ago, I began researching and recalling the details of this crucial part of my professional life—which inevitably touches upon my personal life—and was reminded why I did stand-up and why I walked away.

In a sense, this book is not an autobiography but a biography, because I am writing about someone I used to know. Yes, these events are true, yet sometimes they seemed to have happened to someone else, and I often felt like a curious onlooker or someone trying to remember a dream. I ignored my stand-up career for twenty-five years, but now, having finished this memoir, I view this time with surprising warmth. One can have, it turns out, an affection for the war years.

Coffee and Confusion

ON A HUMID MONDAY NIGHT in the summer of 1965, after finding an eight-dollar hotel room in the then economically friendly city of San Francisco, I lugged my banjo and black, hard-shell prop case ten sweaty blocks uphill to the Coffee and Confusion, where I had signed up to play for free. The club was tiny and makeshift, decorated with chairs, tables, a couple of bare lightbulbs, and nothing else. I had romanticized San Francisco as an exotic destination, away from friends and family and toward mystery and adventure, so I often drove my twenty-year-old self up from Los Angeles to audition my fledgling comedy act at a club or to play banjo on the street for tips. I would either sleep in my VW van, camp

5

out in Golden Gate Park, pay for a cheap hotel, or snag a free room in a Haight-Ashbury Victorian crash pad by making an instant friend. At this point, my act was a catchall, cobbled together from the disparate universes of juggling, comedy, banjo playing, weird bits I'd written in college, and magic tricks. I was strictly Monday-night quality, the night when, traditionally, anyone could get up to perform. All we entertainers knew Mondays were really audition nights for the club.

The Coffee and Confusion, ca. 1965.

I walked past Broadway and Columbus, where Lawrence Ferlinghetti's ramshackle City Lights Books was jam-packed with thin small-press publications offering way-out poetry and reissues of long-ago-banned erotic novels. Around the corner on Broadway was Mike's Pool

Hall, where bikers and hippies first laid eyes on each other, unsure whether they should beat each other up or just smoke pot and forget about it. Steps away was the hungry i, a nightclub that had launched a thousand careers, including those of the Smothers Brothers, the Kingston Trio, and Lenny Bruce, but I had to trudge on by. Just up Columbus, I passed the Condor, the first of a sudden explosion of topless clubs, where Carol Doda, in a newfangled bathing suit that exposed her recently inflated basketball breasts, descended from the ceiling on a grand piano that was painted virginal white. This cultural mélange—and the growing presence of drugs—made the crowded streets of North Beach simmer with toxic vitality.

The Coffee and Confusion was nearby on Grant Avenue, a street dotted with used-clothing stores and incense shops. I nervously entered the club, and Ivan Ultz, the show runner, slotted me into the lineup. I lingered at the back, waiting for my turn, and surveyed the audience of about fifteen people. They were arrayed in patchwork jeans with tie-dyed tops, and the room was thick with an illegal aroma. In the audience was a street poet, dressed in rags and bearded like a yeti, who had a plastic machine gun that shot Ping-Pong balls, which he unloaded on performers he didn't like. I was still untouched by the rapidly changing fashion scene; my short hair and conservative clothes weren't going to help me with this crowd.

Ivan introduced me. My opening line, "Hello. I'm Steve Martin, and I'll be out here in a minute," was met

7

with one lone chuckle. I struggled through the first few minutes, keeping a wary eye on Mr. Ping-Pong Ball, and filled in the dead air with some banjo tunes that went just okay. I could see Ivan standing nearby, concerned. I began to strum the banjo, singing a song that I told the audience my grandmother had taught me:

Be courteous, kind, and forgiving.
Be gentle and peaceful each day.
Be warm and human and grateful,
And have a good thing to say.

Be thoughtful and trustful and childlike,
Be witty and happy and wise.
Be honest and love all your neighbors,
Be obsequious, purple, and clairvoyant.

Be pompous, obese, and eat cactus.
Be dull and boring and omnipresent.
Criticize things you don't know about.
Be oblong and have your knees removed.

Be sure to stop at stop signs,
And drive fifty-five miles an hour.
Pick up hitchhikers foaming at the mouth,
And when you get home get a master's degree in
geology.

8
—

Be tasteless, rude, and offensive.
Live in a swamp and be three-dimensional.
Put a live chicken in your underwear.
Go into a closet and suck eggs.

Then I said, "Now, everyone," and I repeated the entire thing, adding in:

Ladies only!: Never make love to Bigfoot.
Men only!: Hello, my name is Bigfoot.

Not many people sang along.

I thought I was dead, but I wasn't. "And now," I announced, "the napkin trick." Unfolding a paper napkin, I grandly displayed it on both sides, held it up to my face, and stuck my wet tongue through it. I bowed deeply, as though what I had just done was unique in the history of show business. No Ping-Pong balls came my way, only a nice curious laugh that perked up the rest of my show and seemed to make the audience think that what they were seeing might be okay.

I got word from the club's owner, Sylvia Fennell, that the Coffee and Confusion would like to try me for a week as an opening act. Sylvia was a tough but likable New Yorker who had moved west to enter the nightclub business and whose width, height, and depth were the same measurement. She didn't know much about show business, having once told a ventriloquist to move the

9

dummy closer to the microphone. She was, however, savvy about the bottom line, as evidenced by a sign in the kitchen that said: ANYONE GIVING MONEY TO JANIS JOPLIN BEFORE HER LAST SET IS FIRED! AND IF THEY ARE A CUSTOMER, THEY'RE 86'ED! Later, I found out that the main reason I was hired was because I was a member of the musicians' union, which I joined only because I thought I had to be in at least one performers' union, and the musicians' was the cheapest. Sylvia had been told that if she didn't hire a union worker, pronto, the place would be shut down.

The night of my first appearance, Gaylord the bartender—the separate syllables of his name correctly described his sexual orientation and his demeanor—came to me and said it was time to start. "But," I said as I waved my hand to indicate the stone-empty club, "there's nobody here." He pointed to the large window that looked onto the sidewalk, and explained that my job was to be onstage so passersby could see a show going on and be lured in. I said that I wasn't a singer, I was a comedian, and doing comedy for absolutely no one posed a problem. So? he implied. Dave Archer, the amiable doorman, seconded him, telling me that this was the way the evening always began, so I went onstage and started talking. Talking to no one. The first couple who walked through the door did a whiplash scan of the vacant room and immediately left. But more than a few came in, looked around, saw nobody, shrugged an "Oh well," and sat down, especially after Dave offered them a free coffee.

The cheapness of the place gave me some opportunity for laughs. The lights were controlled with wall switches just behind the performer. Saying I wanted a "mood change," I gave an imperious order to the light man, who, the audience soon realized, was me. I reached back and twiddled the rheostat while feigning indignation.

One night I started a serious banjo tune and, sensing the audience's boredom, stopped and said, "I like to keep the laughs rolling even while I'm playing. . . ." I reached down to my prop table and put on my arrow-through-the-head, purchased on a whim at a Hollywood Boulevard magic store, and finished the song. Then I forgot to take it off. Every earnest thing I said was contradicted and deflated by this silly novelty. Sylvia Fennell's advice about the arrow—which was to become my most famous prop—was "Lose it."

I had a strong closer, an absurdist version of a balloon-animal act in which all the balloon animals were unrecognizable. I would end up with the balloons on my head, nose glasses on my face, and bunny ears. The point was to look as stupid as possible, then pause thoughtfully and say, "And now I'd like to get serious for a moment. I know what you're thinking. You're thinking, 'Oh, this is just another banjo-magic act.'"

I was contracted to be onstage for twenty-five minutes. I had a solid ten minutes, and the rest of my material

11
—

was unreliable. If I got some laughs, I could almost make it, but if the audience was dead, my twenty-five-minute show would shrink to about twelve. Afraid of falling short, I ad-libbed, wandered around the audience, talked to patrons, joked with waitresses, and took note of anything unusual that was happening in the crowd and addressed it for laughs, in the hope of keeping my written material in reserve so I could fill my time quota. The format stuck. Years later, it was this pastiche element that made my performances seem unstructured and modern.

That week at the Coffee and Confusion, something started to make sense. My act, having begun three years earlier as a conventional attempt to enter regular show business, was becoming a parody of comedy. I was an entertainer who was playing an entertainer, a not so good one, and this embryonic notion drove me to work on other material in that vein.

After my last show on Sunday, I walked a few doors up to the Coffee Gallery, another Grant Avenue folk club, and sat alone in an empty showroom. On the jukebox was the haunting voice of Frank Sinatra singing ". . . When I was seventeen, it was a very good year." Each successive stanza advanced the narrator by a decade, causing me to reflect on something I could not possibly reflect on: my future. The next song was the Beatles' "Norwegian Wood," and its modal tones underscored the moody darkness. I felt an internal stillness, much like the moment of

12

silence a performer seeks before he goes onstage. I know now why this memory has stuck with me so vividly. My ties to home were broken, I had a new group of friends, I was loose and independent, I had my first job where I slept in a hotel at night instead of my own bed. I was about to start my life.

Comedy Through the Airwaves

MY FATHER WANTED TO BE AN ACTOR and my mother hated the Texas heat, so in 1950, when I was five years old, our family moved from Waco to Hollywood. To maintain family ties, we motored between Texas and California several times over the next few years. On these road trips, I was introduced to comedy. As evening closed around us, my father would turn on the car radio, and with my sister, Melinda, and me nestled in the backseat, we would listen to Bob Hope, Abbott and Costello, the hilarious but now exiled Amos 'n' Andy, and the delight that was *The Jack Benny Program*. These were only voices, heard but unseen, yet they were vivid and vital characters in our imaginations. We laughed out loud as our tubby

Our family in a Texas diner, ca. 1949. Me, my mother, my father, and Melinda. I don't know who the woman in the middle is, unless we happened to be having lunch with Virginia Woolf.

Nash Airflyte glided down the isolated southwestern highways. Listening to comedy was one of the few things our family did together.

My father got a job at the Hollywood Ranch Market on Vine Street, sorting fruit. I was taken to see him act in a play, though I was so young I didn't quite understand what a play was. The performance was at the Callboard Theater on Melrose Place in Los Angeles, and my mother and I sat until the third act, when my father finally came onstage to deliver a drink on a tray and then exit. My father's acting career stopped soon after that, and I had no understanding that he had been interested in show business until I was an adult.

A few months later, we moved from Hollywood to Inglewood, California, and lived in a small bungalow on Venice Way, directly across from Highland Elementary School. This was the site of my first stage performance, where, in kindergarten, I appeared as Rudolph the Red-nosed Reindeer. My matronly teacher, who was probably twenty-two, explained that I would be dressed up like Rudolph and—this was the best part—I would wear a bright red nose made from a Ping-Pong ball. As show time neared, my excitement built. I had the furry suit, the furry feet, and the cardboard antlers. Finally, I asked, "Where's the Ping-Pong ball?" She told me that the Ping-Pong ball would be replaced with lipstick that would be smeared on my nose. What had been delivered as a casual aside, I had taken as a solemn promise; there had never been, I now realized, a serious intent to get a Ping-Pong ball, even though this was my main reason for taking the gig. I went on, did my best Rudolph, and because lipstick doesn't wash off that easily, walked back home hiding my still-crimson nose under my mother's knee-length topcoat. One coat, four legs extending beneath.

I was five years old when television entered the Martin household. A plastic black box wired to a rooftop antenna sat in our living room, and on it appeared what had to be the world's longest continuous showing of B Westerns. I had never seen anything with a plot, so even the corniest, most predictable stories were new to me, and I rode the Wild West by sitting astride a blanket I had placed on the back of an overstuffed chair and gal-

TV!

loped along with the posse. I provided hoof noises by slapping my hands alternately on my thighs and the chair, which made enough variation in the sound effect to give it a bit of authenticity.

The TV also brought into my life two appealing characters named Laurel and Hardy, whom I found clever and gentle, in contrast to the Three Stooges, who were blatant and violent. Laurel and Hardy's work, already thirty years old, had survived the decades with no hint of cobwebs. They were also touching and affectionate, and I believe this is where I got the idea that jokes are funniest when played upon oneself. Jack Benny, always his own victim, had a variety show that turned into a brilliant half-hour situation

18
—

comedy; his likable troupe was now cavorting in my living room, and I was captivated. His slow burn—slower than slow—made me laugh every time. *The Red Skelton Show* aired on Tuesday evening, and I would memorize Red's routines about two pooping seagulls, Gertrude and Heathcliffe, or his bit about how different people walk through a rain puddle, and perform them the next day during Wednesday morning's "sharing time" at my grade school.

My life on Venice Way was spent in close proximity to my mother—the tininess of our house assured it—and I can remember no strife or unpleasantness about our time there. Unpleasantness began to creep into our lives after we moved a few miles away to 720 South Freeman in Inglewood.

MY FATHER, GLENN VERNON MARTIN, died in 1997 at age eighty-three, and afterward his friends told me how much they had loved him. They told me how enjoyable he was, how outgoing he was, how funny and caring he was. I was surprised by these descriptions, because the number of funny or caring words that had passed between my father and me was few. He had evidently saved his vibrant personality for use outside the family. When I was seven or eight years old, he suggested we play catch in the front yard. This offer to spend time together was so rare that I was confused about what I was supposed to do. We tossed the ball back and forth with cheerless formality.

In the second grade, I was in tumbling class. Modern tumbling has nothing to do with tumbling in 1952. Children today spring midair backflips across Olympic-sized arenas right into the arms of Cirque du Soleil talent scouts. Our repertoire included a somersault, a backward somersault, and our highest achievement, the handspring. Next, we would combine the three basic moves into a handspring that turned into a somersault, then into a backward somersault. This might seem impossible to you, but yes, we did it.

One day it was announced that there would be a tumbling competition for second-graders. My father escorted me to school for what seemed like a late-night event, although I look back and realize it couldn't have been past four P.M. Because our challenges were so simple, the contest dragged on, but finally, enough competitors had stumbled into oblivion, and it was down to me and one other boy. After what seemed like hours, my opponent lost his balance during a forward roll. A flurry of seven-year-olds rushed in and hoisted me up on their shoulders, and I was given a golden loving cup. My father and I walked home in the darkness, and he suggested hiding the trophy under his coat to fool my mom. The ruse didn't work, because she saw the glow on my face. This walk home is one of the few times I remember my father and me being close. In our house, my mother was called Mama, but my father was always called Glenn.

As a young woman, my mother, Mary Lee Martin, had a sense of fun that was rarely displayed later in her

My mother in Waco, Texas, ca. 1933.

life. She loved fashion, and in an early snapshot, she is striding the streets of Waco in high style. Melinda and I benefited from her sartorial sense; she was an avid seamstress and made clothes for us that she copied from movie magazines. Starstruck, she proudly saved a newspaper photo of herself in a theater, seated behind the popular actor Van Johnson, and later, at age forty-five, she even managed to get some modeling jobs at local department stores. She impossibly dreamed of a glamorous life. I had always assumed the reason my father ended up selling real estate instead of pursuing acting was that my mother had pressured him to get a real job. But when she was older and I presented this idea to her, she said, "Oh, no, I wanted your father to be a star," and she went on to say that it was he who hadn't followed his dream. My mother was the daughter of a strict Baptist matriarch who barred dancing, dating, and cardplaying, and she must have viewed her marriage to my theatrically inclined father as an exciting alternative to small-town life. But my father overpowered her easily intimidated personality, and she only escaped from one repressive situation into another.

My sister and me in haute couture,
hand-sewn by my mother.

STEVE MARTIN

Though I was just eight years old, I was, like most children in that benign era, allowed to walk alone the few blocks to my new school, Oak Street Elementary, which opened in the 1920s and is still operating today. It has a wee bit of architecture about it, featuring an inner Spanish courtyard with six shady ficus trees. It is directly under the flight path of LAX, and our routine civil defense drills had us convinced that every commercial jet roaring overhead was really a Russian plane about to discharge A-bombs. One rainy day, fooled by a loud clap of thunder, we dived under our desks and covered our heads, believing we were seconds away from annihilation.

At Oak Street School I gave my second performance onstage, which introduced me to an unexpected phenomenon: knocking knees. I had seen knocking knees in animated cartoons but hadn't believed they afflicted small boys. As I got onstage for the Christmas pageant—was I Joseph?—my knees vibrated like a tuning fork. I never experienced the sensation again, but I wonder if I would have preferred it to the chilly pre-show anxiety that I sometimes felt later in my performing career. This mild but persistent adrenal rush beginning days before important performances kept the pounds off and, I swear, kept colds away. I would love to see a scientific study of how many performers come down with the flu twenty-four hours after a show is over, once the body's jazzed-up defenses have collapsed in exhaustion.

23

MY FATHER HAD A RESONANT VOICE, and he liked to sing around the house. He emulated Bing Crosby and Dean Martin, and my mother loved it when he crooned the popular songs of the day. She was a good piano player and kept encouraging me to sing for her, I suppose to find out if I had inherited my father's voice. I was shy at home and kept refusing, but one day after her final push, I agreed. I went to the garage, where I could practice "America the Beautiful" in private. A few hours later, I was ready. She got out the sheet music, placed it on the piano, and I stood before her. After the downbeat, what came out of my mouth was an eight-year-old boy's attempt to imitate his dad's deep baritone. I plunged my voice down as low as it could go, and began to croon the song like Dean Martin might have done at a baseball game. My mother, as much as she wanted to continue, collapsed in laughter and could not stop. Her eyes reddened with tears of affection, and the control she tried to exert over herself made her laugh even more, with her forearm falling on the piano keys as she tried to hide her face from me, filling our small living room with laughter and dissonance. She explained, as kindly as she could, that I was charming, not ridiculous, but I was forever after reluctant to sing in public.

Having been given a few store-bought magic tricks by an uncle, I developed a boy's interest in conjuring and felt a glow of specialness as the sole possessor—at least

24

locally—of its secrets. My meager repertoire of tricks quintupled when my parents gave me a Mysto Magic set, a cherished Christmas gift. The apparatus was flimsy, the instructions indecipherable, and a few of the effects were deeply uninteresting. Out of a box of ten tricks, only four were useful. But even four tricks required practice, so I stood in front of a mirror for hours to master the Linking Rings or the Ball and Vase. My first shows were performed

My mother and father, and my Linking Rings, Christmas 1953.

in my third-grade class, using an upturned apple crate for my magic table. I can still remember the moment when my wooden "billiard balls," intended to multiply and vanish right before your eyes, slipped from between my fingers and bounced around the schoolroom with a humiliating clatter as I scrambled to pick them up. The balls were bright red, and so was I.

My father was the generous one in the family (my mother promoted penny-pinching habits lingering from her Great Depression childhood; her practice of scrimping on household heat nearly froze us into statues on frosty winter mornings). He annoyed my mother by occasionally lending what little leftover money we had to pals in need, but when my mother objected, my father would sternly remind her that they had been able to buy their first house because of the generosity of a family friend. I loved comic books, especially the funny ones, like *Little Lulu,* and man oh man, if Uncle Scrooge was in the latest episode of *Donald Duck,* I was in heaven. My father financed my subscriptions, and I ended up, after one year, owing him five dollars. Though he never dogged me for it, I'm sure he kept this debt on the books to teach me the value of money. As the balance grew, I was nauseated whenever I thought of it. One birthday, he forgave my debt, and I soared with relief. In my adult life, I have never bought anything on credit.

In spite of these sincere efforts at parenting, my father seemed to have a mysterious and growing anger toward me. He was increasingly volatile, and eventually, in my teen years, he fell into enraged silences. I knew that money issues plagued him and that we were always dependent on the next hypothetical real estate sale, and perhaps this was the source of his anger. But I suspect that as his show business dream slipped further into the sunset, he chose to blame his family who needed food, shelter, and attention. Though my sister seemed to escape his wrath, my mother grew more and more submissive to my father in order to avoid his temper. Timid and secretive, she whispered her thoughts to me with the caveat "Now, don't tell anyone I said that," filling me with a belief, which took years to correct, that it was dangerous to express one's true opinion. Melinda, four years older than I, always went to a different school, and a sibling bond never coalesced until decades later, when she phoned me and said, "I want to know my brother," initiating a lasting communication between us.

I was punished for my worst transgressions by spankings with switches or a paddle, a holdover from any Texas childhood of that time, and when my mother warned, "Just wait till Glenn gets home," I would be sick with fear, dreading nightfall, dreading the moment when he would walk through the door. His growing moodiness made each episode of punishment more unpredictable—and hence, more frightening—and once, when I was about nine years old, he went too far. That evening, his mood was ominous as we indulged in a rare family treat, eating

27

our Birds Eye frozen TV dinners in front of the television. My father muttered something to me, and I responded with a mumbled "What." He shouted, "You heard me," thundered up from his chair, pulled his belt out of its loops, and inflicted a beating that seemed never to end. I curled my arms around my body as he stood over me like a titan and delivered the blows. The next day I was covered in welts and wore long pants and sleeves to hide them at school. This was the only incident of its kind in our family. My father was never physically abusive toward my mother or sister and he was never again physically extreme with me. However, this beating and his worsening tendency to rages directed at my mother—which I heard in fright through the thin walls of our home—made me resolve, with icy determination, that only the most formal relationship would exist between my father and me, and for perhaps thirty years, neither he nor I did anything to repair the rift.

The rest of my childhood, we hardly spoke; there was little he said to me that was not critical, and there was little I said back that was not terse or mumbled. When I graduated from high school, he offered to buy me a tuxedo. I refused because I had learned from him to reject all aid and assistance; he detested extravagance and pleaded with us not to give him gifts. I felt, through a convoluted logic, that in my refusal, I was being a good son. I wish now that I had let him buy me a tuxedo, that I had let him be a dad. Having cut myself off from him, and by association the rest of the family, I was incurring psychological debts that would come due years later in the guise of romantic misconnections and a wrong-headed quest for solitude.

I have heard it said that a complicated childhood can lead to a life in the arts. I tell you this story of my father and me to let you know I am qualified to be a comedian.

Disneyland

A WIDE SWATH OF our Inglewood neighborhood was scheduled to be flattened by the impending construction of the San Diego freeway. The steamrollers were soon to be barreling down on our little house, so the search was on for a new place to live. My father's decision profoundly affected my life. Orange County, California, forty-five minutes south of Inglewood, was a real estate boomtown created from the sprawl of Los Angeles. It consisted of interlocking rectangles of orange groves and tract homes and was perfectly suited to my father's profession. Housing developments rose out of the ground like spring wells, changing the color of the landscape from desert brown to lawn green, and my parents purchased a brand-new tract home for sixteen

31

thousand dollars. I was ten years old when my family moved from complicated and historic Los Angeles to uncomplicated and nonhistoric Garden Grove, where the sky was blue and vast but without the drama of Wyoming, just a flat dead sky of ease. Everything from our toes to the horizon was the same, except for the occasional massive and regal oak tree that had defied the developer's scythe. This area of Orange County gleamed with newness, and the move enabled me to place my small hand on Opportunity's doorknob.

In the summer of 1955, Disneyland opened in Anaheim, California, on a day so sweltering the asphalt on Main Street was as soft as a yoga mat. Two-inch headlines announced the event as though it were a victory at sea. A few months later, when a school friend told me that kids our age were being hired to sell Disneyland guidebooks on weekends and in the summer, I couldn't wait. I pedaled my bicycle the two miles to Disneyland, parked it in the bike rack—locks were unnecessary—and looked up to see a locomotive from yesteryear, its whistle blowing loudly and its smokestack filling the air with white steam, chugging into the turn-of-the-century depot just above a giant image of Mickey Mouse rendered in vibrantly colored flowers. I went to the exit, told a hand-stamper that I was applying for a job, and was directed toward a souvenir stand a few steps inside the main gate. I spoke with a cigar-chomping vendor named Joe and told him my résumé: no experience at anything. This must have impressed Joe, because I was issued a candy-striped shirt, a garter for my sleeve, a vest with a watch pocket, a straw boater hat, and a stack of guidebooks to be sold for twenty-five cents each, from which I was to receive the enormous sum of two cents per book. The two dollars in cash I earned that day made me feel like a millionaire.

Guidebooks were sold only in the morning, when thousands of people poured through the gates. By noon I was done, but I didn't have to leave. I had free admission to the park. I roamed through the Penny Arcade, watched the Disneyland Band as they marched around the plaza, and even found an "A" ticket in the street, allowing me to choose between the green-and-gold-painted streetcar or the surrey ride up Main Street. Because I wisely kept on my little outfit, signifying that I was an official employee, and maybe because of the look of longing on my face, I was given a free ride on the Tomorrowland rocket to the moon, which blasted me into the cosmos. I passed by Mr. Toad and Peter Pan rides, toured pirate ships and Western forts. Disneyland, and the idea of it, seemed so glorious that I believed it should be in some faraway, impossible-to-visit Shangri-la, not two miles from the house where I was about to grow up. With its pale blue castle flying pennants emblazoned with a made-up Disney family crest, its precise gardens and horse-drawn carriages maintained to jewel-box perfection, Disneyland was my Versailles.

I became a regular employee, age ten. I blazed short-cuts through Disneyland's maze of pathways, finding the

33

most direct route from the Chicken of the Sea pirate ship to the Autopia, or the back way to Adventureland from Main Street. I learned speed-walking, and I could slip like a water moccasin through dense throngs of people, a technique I still use at airports and on the sidewalks of Manhattan. Though my mother provided fifty cents for lunch (the Carnation lunch counter offered a grilled cheese sandwich for thirty-five cents and a large cherry phosphate with a genuine red-dye-number-two cherry for fifteen cents), the big difference in my life was that I was self-reliant and funded. I was so proud to be employed that some years later—still at Disneyland—I harbored a secret sense of superiority over my teenage peers who had suntans, because I knew it meant they weren't working.

In Frontierland, I was fascinated by a true cowboy named Eddie Adamek, who twirled lariats and pitched his homemade product, a prefab lasso that enabled youngsters to make perfect circles just like their cowboy heroes. Eddie, I discerned, was living with a woman not his wife, the 1955 equivalent of devil worship. But I didn't mind, because his patronage enabled me to learn rope tricks, including the Butterfly, Threading the Needle, and the Skip-Step. A few years later, after my tenure as guide-book salesman ended—perhaps at thirteen I was too old—I became Eddie's trick-rope demonstrator, fitting in as much work as I could around my C-average high school studies.

34

In my mapping of the Disney territory, two places captivated me. One was Merlin's Magic Shop, just inside the Fantasyland castle gate, where a young and funny magician named Jim Barlow sold and demonstrated magic tricks. The other was Pepsi-Cola's Golden Horseshoe Revue in Frontierland, where Wally Boag, the first comedian I ever saw in person, plied a hilarious trade of gags and offbeat skills such as gun twirling and balloon animals, and brought the house down when he turned his wig around backward. He wowed every audience every time.

The theater, built with Disneyland's dedication to craftsmanship, had a horseshoe-shaped interior adorned with lush gay-nineties decor. Oak tables and chairs crowded the saloon's main floor, and a spectacular mirrored bar with a gleaming foot rail ran along one side. Polished brass lamps with real flames gave off an orangey glow, and on the stage hung a plush golden curtain tied back with a thickly woven cord. A balcony lined with steers' horns looped around the interior, and customers dangled their arms and heads over the railing during the show. Four theater boxes stood on either side of the stage, where VIPs would be seated ceremoniously behind a velvet rope. Young girls in low-cut dance-hall dresses served paper cups brimming with Pepsi that seemed to have an exceptionally stinging carbonated fizz, and the three-piece band made the theater jump with liveliness. In the summer the powerful air-conditioning made it a welcome icebox.

35
—

The admission price, always free to everyone, made me a regular. Here I had my first lessons in performing, though I never was on the stage. I absorbed Wally Boag's timing, saying his next line in my head ("When they operated on Father, they opened Mother's male"), and took the audience's response as though it were mine. I studied where the big laughs were, learned how Wally got the small ones, and saw tiny nuances that kept the thing alive between lines. Wally shone in these performances, and in my first shows, I tried to imitate his amiable casualness. My fantasy was that one day Wally would be sick with the flu, and a desperate stage manager would come out and ask the audience if there was an adolescent boy who could possibly fill in.

Merlin's Magic Shop was the next best thing to the cheering audiences at the Golden Horseshoe. Tricks were demonstrated in front of crowds of two or three people, and twenty-year-old Jim Barlow took the concept of a joke shop far beyond what the Disney brass would have officially allowed, except it was clear that the customers enjoyed his kidding. Coiled springs of snakes shot out of fake peanut-brittle cans, attacking the unsuspecting customer who walked through the door. Jim's greeting to browsers was, "Can I take your money—I mean help you?" After a sale, he would say loudly, "This trick is guaranteed! . . . to break before you get home." Like Wally, Jim was genuinely funny, and his broad smile and innocent blond flattop smoothed the way for his prankster style. I

36
—

loitered in the shop so often that Jim and I became buddies as I memorized his routines, and I wanted more than ever to be a magician.

The paraphernalia sold in the magic store was exotic, and I was dazzled by the tricks' secret mechanics. The Sucker Die Box, with its tricky false fronts and gimmicked door pulls, thrilled me. At home, I would peruse magic catalogs for hours. I was spellbound by the graphics of another era, unchanged since the thirties, of tubes that produced silks, water bowls that poured endlessly, and magic wands that did nothing. I dreamed of owning color-changing scarves and amazing swords that could spear the selected card when the deck was thrown into the air. I read advertising pamphlets from distant companies in Ohio that offered collapsible opera hats, pre-owned tuxedos, and white-tipped canes. I had fantasies of levitation and awesome power and, with no Harry Potter to be compared to, my store-bought tricks could go a long way toward making me feel special. With any spare money I had, I bought tricks, memorized their accompanying standard patter, and assembled a magic show that I would perform for anyone who would watch, mostly my parents and their tolerant bridge partners.

One afternoon I was in the audience at the Golden Horseshoe, sipping my Pepsi and mouthing along with Wally Boag, when I blacked out and collapsed. I remember my head striking the table. A few seconds later, I was sitting back up but unnerved. Nobody noticed, but I re-

I loved my derby hat and cane,
both purchased by mail.

ported this incident to my mother, and she called Dr. Kus-
nitz, perhaps Orange County's only Jewish doctor, who
lived next door. "What was it?" he asked. "It was a thump
in my chest," I said. Tests confirmed I had a heart murmur,
more spookily expressed as a prolapsed mitral valve, a
mostly benign malady that was predicted to go away as I
aged. It did, but it planted in me a seed of hypochondria
that poisonously bloomed years later.

After poor sales ended my trick-roping days, I spent a year working away from the action, in the sheet-metal-gray storage room of Tiki's Tropical Imports in Adventureland, where I pinned finger-piercing price tags onto straw hats (I'm sure my bloody screams alarmed the nearby dock loaders). On my infrequent trips to the actual store, I was entertained by a vibrant Biloxi-born store manager named Irene, who, I now realize, was probably the first neurotic I ever met. Her favorite saying—"Well, excuse me for livin'!"—stuck in my head. I had heard rumors of a job opening up at the magic shop, and longing to be free of the sunless warehouse, I went over and successfully applied, making that day the happiest of my life so far. I began my show business career a few days later, at age fifteen, in August 1960. I stood behind a counter eight hours a day, shuffling Svengali decks, manipulating Wizard decks and Mental Photography cards, and performing the Cups and Balls trick on a rectangle of padded green felt. A few customers would gather, usually a young couple on a date, or a mom and dad with kids. I tried my first jokes—all lifted from Jim's funny patter—and had my first audience that wasn't friends or family. My weekends and holidays were now spent in long hours at Disneyland, made possible by lax child labor laws and my high school, which assigned no homework. At closing time, I would stock the shelves, sweep the floor, count out the register, and then bicycle home in the dark.

At the magic shop.

The magic shop purveyed such goodies as the arrow-through-the-head and nose glasses, props I turned into professional assets later on. Posted behind the scenes, too risqué for Disneyland's tourists, was a little gag postcard that had been printed in Japan. It said, "Happy Feet," and featured the outline of the bottoms of four feet, two pointed up, two pointed down. After I studied it for about an hour, Jim Barlow explained that it was the long-end view of a couple making love.

There were two magic shops—the other was on Main Street—and I ran between them as necessary. In the Main Street store, there was a booth, really an alcove, where you could get your name printed in a headline, WANTED, HORSE THIEF, YOUR NAME HERE, and I mastered the soon-to-be-useless art of hand typesetting. The proprietor, Jim—a different Jim—laughed at me because I insisted on wearing gardening gloves while I worked with the printing press. I couldn't let the ink stain my hands; it would look unsightly when I was demonstrating cards. At the print shop I learned my first life lesson. One day I was particularly gloomy, and Jim asked me what the matter was. I told him my high school girlfriend (for all of two weeks) had broken up with me. He said, "Oh, that'll happen a lot." The knowledge that this horrid grief was simply a part of life's routine cheered me up almost instantly.

Merlin's was run by Leo Behnke, a fine card and coin manipulator who was the first person to let me in on the inner secrets of magic, and who endorsed a strict code of practice and discipline that I took to heart. But Leo had another quality that transfixed me. He handled cards with delicacy; there was a rhythm to his movements that was mildly hypnotic. He could shuffle the deck without ever lifting it from the tabletop: After an almost invisible riffle, every card was interlaced exactly with the next, a perfect shuffle. Then, with the elegance of Fred Astaire, he squared the cards by running his fingers smoothly around the edges of the deck. Leo taught me his perfect shuffle (called the faro shuffle), which I perfected a mere

41
—

four months later, and I squared the deck just like he did. I enjoyed making the sleights imperceptible and moving my fingers around the cards with Leo's grace and ease. A magician's hands are often hiding things, and I learned that stillness can be as deceptive as motion. It was my first experience with the pleasure and subtlety of physical expression, and I became aware of the potency of movement.

Because I was demonstrating tricks eight to twelve hours a day, I got better and better. I could even duplicate the effects of trick decks with a regular deck. I was able to afford more professional equipment, including, at a price of four dollars and fifty cents, the Zombie, a floating silver ball that danced behind a silk scarf to bewildering effect. I put together a magic act, complete with music, that required a friend to put the needle down on a record at exactly the right moment, in exactly the right groove. Jim Barlow connected me to a network of desperate Cub Scout troops seeking entertainment, and the minuscule prestige from my magic shop gig enabled me to work for free or sometimes for five dollars at the local Kiwanis Club. I was now performing at the hectic pace of one show every two or three months. Later in life, I wondered why the Kiwanis Club or the Rotary Club, comprised of grown men, would hire a fifteen-year-old boy magician to entertain at their dinners. Only one answer makes sense: out of the goodness of their hearts.

Claude Plum, a suspender-wearing oddnik who, among

Performing for Cub Scouts.

other things, collected thousands of B-movie stills from the 1940s, wrote a mimeographed in-house newsletter for Disneyland and supplied gags for Wally Boag: "I'm in the dark side of the cattle business." "Do you rustle?" "Only when I wear taffeta shorts." He would lend me his copies of Robert Orben's joke books, filled with musty one-liners from other comedians' acts, but to me they were as new as sunrise. These books were like the Bible and I scoured them for usable passages. For five dollars, a major investment, I hired Claude to write some material for my floating silver ball routine: "With the advent of the space age," I squeaked, "scientists have been searching for a metal that can defy gravity. . . . "

The magic shop put me in daily contact with people, and when I was fifteen, there was only one kind of people: girls. I have a clear memory of standing behind the counter watching a girl in shorts turn away from me, and being confronted by the alarmingly pleasant sight of her rear end and all its curvy virtues. My body flooded with chemistry, and the female behind was instantly added to my growing list of turn-ons, which up till then included only faces, hair, and that which I will call brassieres, because actual breasts were still unseen and never experienced. The Main Street store was run by Aldini the Magician—real name Alex Weiner—a mustachioed, tart-tongued spiel-meister who taught me all the Yiddish words I know, including the invaluable *tuchis* (meaning "ass"), which he used as a code word to indicate that a sexy girl had come into the shop.

I did have a life outside Disneyland. I had been attending Rancho Alamitos High School, but in the fall of 1962, redistricting moved me across town to Garden Grove High School, where I was happy to discard my old personality and adopt a new one defined by the word of the day, "nonconformist." Of course, the difference between my old personality and my new personality was probably imperceptible, so I was lucky to have all-new classmates who would not remember my old conformist ways.

On my first day of school, the student body was called together for an assembly, and this was when I saw the

44

face of God. The Don Wash Auditorium seated fifteen hundred people, and its interior narrowed like a funnel to focus all eyes on its polished hardwood stage. The proscenium was framed by heavy velvet curtains, and the acoustics were—and still are—brilliant and sharp, making microphones unnecessary. I sat in the audience, looking up at the stage, surrounded by high-energy, adolescent chatter. The house lights dimmed dramatically, and when the crisp ice-blue spotlight illuminated center stage in anticipation of parting curtains and grand entrances, I knew I wanted to be up there rather than down here.

When Claude Plum asked me to appear in a vaudeville show featuring Wally Boag, coincidentally staged at this auditorium, my heart leaped. I was to perform a five-minute act, billed as "Steve Martin: Youth and Magic," in an evening show for Wally's fans. The programs appeared from the printer with the perfect prescient typo: "Steve Martin: Mouth and Magic." I couldn't judge how it went, since it was my first show in front of a sizable audience, but I don't remember a standing ovation. Claude Plum appeared in the program, too, but he listed his name as Clyde Primm in order to escape creditors. Years later, I ran into him working at Larry Edmunds's rare-book store on Hollywood Boulevard. Claude was still weird and mysterious, a bit of a pigpen, still with a one-inch stub of smoldering cigarette pursed in his lips, still collecting artifacts of forties film noir.

45
—

The daily excitement of my life at Disneyland and high school was in stark contrast to my life at home. Silent family dinners, the general taboo on free talk and opinion, my father's unpredictable temper, and the stubborn grudges I collected and held toward him meant that the family never gelled. But when I was away from home, my high school pals and I enjoyed endless conversation and laughter, and my enthusiasm for what I was doing—working at Disneyland, clowning with friends, and being swept up in the early rock and roll of AM radio—made life seem joyful and limitless. When I moved out of the house at eighteen, I rarely called home to check up on my parents or tell them how I was doing. Why? The answer shocks me as I write it: I didn't know I was supposed to.

THINGS WERE CHANGING at the magic shop. Leo Behnke left to consult on a television show, and our store needed a new manager. Leo's replacement was a fortunate choice for me. Dave Steward, emaciated, lanky, and deadpan, was an actual former vaudevillian who had worked the circuits with a magic act. He went by the name Lord Chesterfield, later changed to David and Company because, he said, the "company" implied two people, and he could ask for more money. His act had been that of a stone-faced, bungling magician, which appealed to me because Jim Barlow's and my hero at the time was the king of bungling magicians, Carl Ballantine, whose legendary appearances on *The Ed Sullivan Show* nudged every young magician toward comedy.

Dave Steward's vaudeville act had involved an ordinary-looking violin that he was always about to play but never did. His big finish, enabled by old-world craftsmanship, was its instantaneous transformation into a bouquet of flowers. One day he brought his trick violin to the store to share with this sixteen-year-old boy. He flicked a hidden switch, and I watched as the violin changed into a colorful bouquet of feather-flowers. Nice, but then he showed me his opening joke: He walked from behind the counter and stood on the floor of the magic shop, announcing, "And now, the glove into dove trick!" He threw a white magician's glove into the air. It hit the floor and lay there. He stared at it and then went on to the next trick. It was the

47

Dave Steward's vaudeville publicity photo.

STEVE MARTIN

first time I had ever seen laughter created out of absence. I found this gag so funny that I asked permission to use it in my youthful magic act, and he said yes.

He told me another bit. He would take out a white handkerchief, pretend to mop his brow, and then, thanks to a rubber ball sewn into the cloth, absentmindedly bounce it on the floor. I didn't really get the joke, but the concept stuck. I took a high-bounce juggling ball and sewed it inside a realistic-looking cloth rabbit. Producing the bunny from a tube painted with Chinese symbols, I would say, "And now, a live bouncing baby rabbit!" Then, to everyone's shock and eventual laughter, I would bounce the rabbit on the floor. I had my first original gag.

Dave Steward's stories intrigued me, and I developed an interest in the history of vaudeville. I read up on the subject, studying Joe Laurie's book *Vaudeville,* and was captivated by its descriptions of each old-time act. It mentioned the Cherry Sisters, and it was here that I first heard an act described as "so bad it was good." The five screeching sisters elicited boos and vegetables from the audience and yet still made it to Broadway, a concept that the off-pitch singer Mrs. Miller succeeded with in the sixties and that Andy Kaufman took to the limit in the eighties. My interests widened to carnival scams, thanks to the nearby Long Beach Pike and its boardwalk games and sideshow featuring Zuzu the Monkey Girl; Electra (a woman who could light lightbulbs in her bare hand); and a two-headed baby

49

resting in formaldehyde that was actually a convincing rubber facsimile. There was also a roller coaster called the Cyclone Racer, whose behemoth wooden skeleton extended out over the sea. I was hoping the carnies would let me in on their secrets, but they never did. Maybe it was my Ivy League button-down shirts that kept them from thinking I was one of them.

The Main Street shop sold magic books. Rarely purchased, they gathered dust on a high shelf. A yellow cover caught my eye, and this book turned out to be more important to me than *The Catcher in the Rye*. It was Dariel Fitzkee's *Showmanship for Magicians*, first published in 1943. A terse Internet bio of Mr. Fitzkee (who turned out, coincidentally, to be a distant relative by marriage) describes him this way:

Born in Annawan, Illinois. Pen name of Dariel Fitzroy. Acoustical engineer in San Rafael, California. Semi-pro magician. Toured an unsuccessful full-evening show 1939–40. Reportedly dropped magic in disgust.

Showmanship for Magicians is a handbook meant to turn amateurs into professionals. Its subtitle is *Complete Discussions of Audience Appeals and Fundamentals of Showmanship and Presentation*. I held my first copy and solemnly turned the pages, reading each sentence so slowly that it's a miracle I could remember what the verb was. The cover was plain-faced—like a secret manifesto

50
—

that should be hidden under your mattress—and the pages were as thick as rags. Fitzkee starts by denigrating the current state of magic, saying it is old-fashioned. Though published in 1943, this statement contains an enduring truth. All entertainment is or is about to become old-fashioned. There is room, he implies, for something new. To a young performer, this is a relief. My references were all in the past, and in just one chapter, these roots were severed, or at least choked. Fitzkee then goes on to break down a show into elements such as Music, Rhythm, Comedy, Sex Appeal, Personality, and Selling Yourself, and he concludes that attention to each is vital and necessary. Why not throw everything in the book at the audience, like an opera does? Costumes, lights, music, everything? He also talks about something that was to land on me with a thud six years later: the importance of originality. "So what," I thought at the time. "Who cares?"

Following the advice in *Showmanship for Magicians*, I kept scrupulous records of how each gag played after my local shows for the Cub Scouts or Kiwanis Club. "Excellent!" or "Big laugh!" or "Quiet," I would write in the margins of my Big Indian tablet; then I would summarize how I could make the show better next time. I was still motivated to do a magic show with standard patter, but the nice response to a few gags had planted a nagging thought that contradicted my magical goal: They love it when the tricks don't work. I started to think that the

51

for act.

Notes

Leave out unessasary ~~and~~ jokes, change
patter for Sq. Circle, Relax, dont shake,

Hindu Rope
Hippty Hops
Routine w/ 20th century silks w/ Kid.
   went Real good, work on and put
in reg. act.

   En Rapport
   Get a conection with the audience like
at work. length act.

   Show went over good in spite of all
corrections, Charge money

   Good gag.

The show was for Fed-mart. when
Brakaway wand broke I said " Gee, I
got it at C.M.A. Too"

My performing notes, from age fifteen, complete with misspellings.

future of a serious magician was limited. Plus, I was
priced out of the market by the impossible cost of
advanced stage illusions: Sawing a Lady in Half, two hundred dollars. By doing comedy, however, I could be more
like Stan Laurel and Jack Benny, more like Wally Boag.
I was still using Claude's somber introduction to my
floating silver ball routine, but I added a twist at the end

52

of the long-winded speech: "And now, ladies and gentlemen, the toilet float trick."

My time at the magic shop gave me a taste of performing and convinced me that I never wanted to wait on customers again. I didn't have the patience; my smile was becoming plastered on. I then crossed all kinds of jobs off my list of potentials, such as waiting tables or working in stores or driving trucks: How could my delicate fingertips, now dedicated to the swift execution of the Two-handed Pass, clutch the heavy, callus-inducing steering wheel of a ten-ton semi?

But there was a problem. At age eighteen, I had absolutely no gifts. I could not sing or dance, and the only acting I did was really just shouting. Thankfully, perseverance is a great substitute for talent. Having been motivated by Earl Scruggs's rendition of "Foggy Mountain Breakdown," I had learned, barely, to play the banjo. I had taught myself by slowing down banjo records on my turntable and picking out the songs note by note, with a helpful assist from my high school friend John McEuen, already an accomplished player. The only place to practice without agonizing everyone in the house was in my car, parked on the street with the windows rolled up, even in the middle of August. Also, I could juggle passably, a feat I had learned from the talented Fantasyland court jester Christopher Fair (who could juggle five balls while riding a high unicycle) and which I practiced in my backyard using heavy wooden croquet balls that would clack

53

against each other, pinching my swollen fingers in between. Despite a lack of natural ability, I did have the one element necessary to all early creativity: naïveté, that fabulous quality that keeps you from knowing just how unsuited you are for what you are about to do.

After high school graduation, I halfheartedly applied to and was accepted at Santa Ana Junior College, where I took drama classes and pursued an unexpected interest in English poetry from Donne to Eliot. I had heard about a theater at Disneyland's friendly, striving rival, Knott's Berry Farm, that needed entertainers with short acts. One afternoon I successfully auditioned with my thin magic act at a small theater on the grounds, making this the second happiest day of my life so far.

My final day at the magic shop, I stood behind the counter where I had pitched Svengali decks and the Incredible Shrinking Die, and I felt an emotional contradiction: nostalgia for the present. Somehow, even though I had stopped working only minutes earlier, my future fondness for the store was clear, and I experienced a sadness like that of looking at a photo of an old, favorite pooch. It was dusk by the time I left the shop, and I was redirected by a security guard who explained that a photographer was taking a picture and would I please use the side exit. I did, and saw a small, thin woman with hacked brown hair aim her large-format camera directly at the dramatically lit castle, where white swans floated in the moat underneath the functioning drawbridge. Almost

54

forty years later, when I was in my early fifties, I purchased that photo as a collectible, and it still hangs in my house. The photographer, it turned out, was Diane Arbus. I try to square the photo's breathtakingly romantic image with the rest of her extreme subject matter, and I assume she saw this facsimile of a castle as though it were a kitsch roadside statue of Paul Bunyan. Or perhaps she saw it as I did: beautiful.

The Bird Cage Theatre

DURING THE 1960s, the five-foot-high hand-painted placard in front of the Bird Cage Theatre at Knott's Berry Farm read WORLD'S GREATEST ENTERTAIMENT. The missing "n" in "entertainment" was overlooked by staff, audience, and visitors for an entire decade. I worked there between the ages of eighteen and twenty-two as an actor in melodramas. Knott's Berry Farm didn't have the flash of its younger sibling, Disneyland, but it was authentic and charming. Knott's Berry Farm began in the 1930s, when Walter and Cordelia Knott put up a roadside berry stand. A few years later, Cordelia opened her chicken-dinner restaurant, and Walter bought pieces of a ghost town and moved the Old West buildings to his burgeoning tourist

57

destination. Squawking peacocks roamed the grounds, and there was a little wooden chapel that played organ music while you stared at a picture of Jesus and watched his eyes magically open.

My first performances for a paying audience were at the Bird Cage, a wooden theater with a canvas roof. Inside, two hundred folding chairs sat on risers, and a thrust Masonite stage sat behind a patch of fake grass. A painted cutout of a birdcage, worthy of a Sotheby's folk art auction, hung over center stage, and painted representations of drapes framed the proscenium. The actors swept the stage, raised and lowered the curtains, cleaned the house of trash, and went out on the grounds pitching the show to visitors strolling around the park. I was being paid two dollars a show, twenty-five shows a week. Even in 1963, the rate was considered low.

The show consisted of a twenty-five-minute melodrama in which the audience was encouraged to cheer the hero and boo the villain. I appeared in *The Bungling Burglar*, performing the role of Hamilton Brainwood, a detective who was attracted to the provocatively named soubrette, Dimples Reardon. Fortunately, I ended up with the virtuous heroine, Angela Trueheart. My opening night was attended by my high school girlfriend, Linda Rasmussen, and her parents, who, it turned out, were more nervous for me than I was. The play was followed by a ten-minute "olio" segment involving two five-minute routines where the actors did their specialties, usually songs or

Performing the olio at the Bird Cage.

short comedy acts. Though I didn't do an olio that night, the Bird Cage was the first place where I was able to work steadily on my magic act, six minutes at a time, four times a day, five on Sunday, for three years.

The Bird Cage was a normal theatrical nuthouse. Missed cues caused noisy pileups in the wings, or a missing prop left us hanging while we ad-libbed excuses to leave the stage and retrieve it. A forgotten line would hang in the dead air, searching for someone, anyone, to say it. The theater was run by Woody Wilson, a dead ringer for W. C. Fields, and a boozer, too, and the likable George Stuart, who, on Saturday night, would entertain the crowd with a monologue that had them roaring: "You're from Tucson? I spent a week there one night!" Four paying customers, in a house that seated two hundred, was officially an audience, so we often did shows to resonating silence. Woody Wilson, on one of these dead afternoons, peed so loudly in the echoing bathroom that it broke up us actors and got laughs from our conservative family audience.

The theater was stocked with genuine characters. Ronnie Morgon, rail thin, would dress up as Lincoln and read the Gettysburg Address for local elementary schools. On a good day, he would show us young lads cheesecake photos of his wife in a leopard-skin bikini, and even at age eighteen, we thought it was weird. There was Joe Carney, a blustery and funny actor who opened the lavatory door from the top to avoid germs. Paul Shackleton

Me, Terri Jo Flynn, Ronnie Morgon, and George Stuart in a publicity photo, though we never got any publicity.

was the son of a preacher and could not tolerate a swear word, but he once laughed till he cried when we sat down under a eucalyptus tree to drink our Cokes and a bird shit on my head. His laughter made me think it was funny, too, and for days we could not look each other in the eye without breaking into uncontrollable hysterics. John Stuart, a talented tenor with a mischievous sense of humor, once secretly put talcum powder in my top hat. Onstage, whenever I popped the hat on or off, a mushroom cloud of smoke bloomed from my head, causing an unscheduled laugh from the audience.

Kathy Westmoreland, another actress at the theater, had attended Garden Grove High School at the same time I did and was the first indisputably talented person

61

I ever met. She sang like the Swedish Nightingale and, later in life, achieved a strange kind of celebrity. As a backup singer for Elvis, she became his confidante and then, quietly, his lover. Years later, after his death, she wrote a book revealing her secret, making her the focus of overwrought Elvis fans.

Kathy and I developed a hillbilly routine, she on washtub bass and I on banjo. It was my first foray into comedy without magic to back me up. She blacked out a tooth, and the act included crossed eyes and corny jokes, and it absolutely killed. We soon ascended to the premier slot for the Bird Cage's olio acts, the Saturday-night nine o'clock performance. The audience would howl and weep and thrash about, and the laughs would double the length of our five-minute show.

We decided to take our act to the Golden Bear for a Monday tryout. The "Bear" was a folk music club in Huntington Beach, California, where all the big names played, including Kenny Rankin, John Mayall, Jackson Browne, and Hoyt Axton (an accomplished performer and songwriter himself—author of the oddly unforgettable lyric "Jeremiah was a bullfrog!"—but it's hard to forget that his mother cowrote "Heartbreak Hotel"). I was smug about presenting our fully broken-in and seemingly invulnerable act. My belief in the inevitability of our success charged me up before, during, and after the show, and it was not until days later when I acknowledged to myself that our debut in the tougher world of real show business had been met with only a polite response. Kathy and I were probably too corny for an exploding folk scene that was producing many serious and spectacular artists. The willing and forgiving audiences at the Bird Cage did not necessarily reflect those at hip folk clubs.

And then there was Stormie.

Stormie Sherk, later to become an enormously successful Christian author and proselytizer under her married name, Stormie Omartian, was beautiful, witty, bright, and filled with an engaging spirit that was not yet holy. We performed in plays together; my role was either the comic or the leading man, depending on the day of the week. She wore antique calico dresses that complemented her strawberry-blond hair and vanilla skin. Soon we were in love and would roam around Knott's in our period clothes and find a period place to sit, mostly by the period church next to the man-made lake, where we would stare endlessly into each other's eyes. We developed a love duet for the Bird Cage in which she would sing "Gypsy Rover" while I accompanied her on the five-string. When she sang the song, the lyric that affected me the most was—believe it or not—"La dee do la dee do dum day." We would talk of a wedding in a lilac-covered dale, and I could fill any conversational gaps with ardent recitations of Keats and Shelley. Finally, the inevitable happened. I was a late-blooming eighteen-year-old when I had my first sexual experience, involving a

63

condom (swiped from my parents' drawer) and the front seat of my car, whose windows became befogged with desire. Later, Stormie wrote in her autobiography that when she was a girl, her severely mentally ill mother would lock her in a dark closet for days, cruelly abusing her. I had no idea.

If Stormie had said I would look good in a burgundy

Stormie, me.

STEVE MARTIN

ball gown, I would have gone out and bought a burgundy ball gown. Instead, she suggested that I read W. Somerset Maugham's *The Razor's Edge*. *The Razor's Edge* is a book about a quest for knowledge. Universal, final, unquestionable knowledge. I was swept up in the book's glorification of learning and the idea that, like a stage magician, I could have secrets possessed by only a few. Santa Ana Junior College offered no philosophy classes, so I immediately applied to Long Beach State College (later renamed the loftier-sounding California State University at Long Beach) and enrolled with a major in philosophy. I paid for schooling out of my Bird Cage wages, aided in my second year by a dean's list scholarship (one hundred eighty dollars a year) achieved through my impassioned studying, fueled by *Razor's Edge* romanticism. I rented a small apartment near school, so small that its street number was 1059 ¹/₄. Stormie eventually moved an hour north to attend UCLA, and we struggled for a while to see each other, but without the metaphor of the nineteenth century to enchant us, we realized that our real lives lay before us, and, painfully for me, we drifted apart.

At the Bird Cage, I formed the soft, primordial core of what became my comedy act. Over the three years I worked there, I strung together everything I knew, including Dave Steward's glove into dove trick, some comedy juggling, a few standard magic routines, a banjo song, and some very old jokes. My act was eclectic, and

65

it took ten more years for me to make sense of it. However, the opportunity to perform four and five times a day gave me confidence and poise. Even though my material had few distinguishing features, the repetition made me lose my amateur rattle.

Catalyzed by the popularity of the folk group the Kingston Trio, small music clubs began to sprout in every unlikely venue. Shopping malls and restaurant cellars now had corner-stage showrooms that sometimes did and sometimes didn't serve alcohol. There were no clubs dedicated to comedy—they did not exist for at least fifteen years—so every comedian was an outsider. The Paradox, in Tustin, was where I first saw the Dillards, a bluegrass group that played hard and made us laugh, too, and featured the whizbang five-string banjo picker Doug Dillard, who looked like a grin on a stick but played with staggering speed and clarity. There was the Rouge et Noir in Seal Beach, where I saw David-Troy (aka David Somerville, aka Diamond Dave), a singer-guitarist who had the ladies swooning and who had been, years earlier, the lead singer on the Diamonds' monster hit "Little Darlin'." I didn't realize I was hearing one of the most famous voices in early rock and roll. At the Mecca, in Buena Park, I saw the up-and-coming comedian Pat Paulsen, who opened with this funny line: "I've had a great life, with the exception of 1959, when, unfortunately, I passed away." (The best opening line I ever heard was from Sam Kinison. In the late eighties, playing the Comedy Store in Los Angeles, he said, "You're going to see a lot of comedians tonight; some will be good, some will be okay. But there's a difference between me and them. Them, you might want to see again sometime." But wait—maybe the best opening line I heard was Richard Pryor's, after he started two hours late in front of a potentially miffed crowd at the Troubadour in Los Angeles. He said simply, "Hope I'm funny.")

Using the Bird Cage as a home base, I flirted with outside work, auditioning for gigs while keeping my class load at school as light as possible. The Prison of Socrates was a music club in the T-shirts-and-shorts beach town of Balboa. The Prison's main star was a charismatic sandal-clad folksinger named Tim Morgon, who was so popular that for several months in Southern California, his record outsold the Beatles' *A Hard Day's Night*. My Monday-night audition at the Prison was marginal, but because the opening acts were usually marginal anyway, I was hired for a weekend tryout. I now had my first job outside Knott's Berry Farm, which presented a particular difficulty. It was one thing to do five minutes at the Bird Cage, or ten minutes at a "hoot," but it was another thing to do twenty minutes for paying customers. Furiously trying to expand the act before my three-day gig, I threw in earnest readings of the poets e. e. cummings, T. S. Eliot, Carl Sandburg, and Stephen Vincent Benét, all aimed at stretching my act to show length. Nobody cared about hearing Eliot and cummings in a nightclub, but the Benét piece, a socko narra-

67

tive poem about a fiddle contest in Georgia, stayed in the act for at least a year until I canned it.

Opening night, I stood in the parking lot behind the club, going over my material and warming up on the banjo. Adjacent to garbage cans and blowing with beach sand, the parking lot was where the opening acts tuned up and rehearsed, as there was no place else to practice out of the audience's earshot. I performed to a sparse crowd, among them my college friend Phil Carey, his brothers, and their dates. How did it go? I have no idea. My only memories of it are the unsettling echo of chairs screeching on the concrete floor as patrons adjusted their seats. After the show, I was informed by my college friends that I had mispronounced the word "incomparable."

I now had two credits, the Bird Cage and the Prison of Socrates—my Disneyland credit was not quite professional—and I was able to land intermittent jobs, among them the Ice House in Pasadena, which had been converted from—guess what—an icehouse. Many earnest folk musicians appeared there, strumming guitars and wearing shirts with puffy sleeves. At the Ice House, I faced a real nightclub audience and performed almost as frequently as I did at the Bird Cage. Three shows a night was standard at these small clubs. Eventually, I ingratiated myself with enough venues that I wondered if I could possibly finance my life without the security of my steady job at Knott's Berry Farm.

68

Having no agent or any hopes of finding one, I could

Onstage at the Ice House, doing my parody
of male models.

not audition for movies or television or even learn where
auditions were held. I didn't know about trade papers—
Variety or *The Hollywood Reporter*—from which I might
have gathered some information. I lived in suburbia at a
time when a one-hour drive to Los Angeles in my first
great car—a white 1957 Chevy Bel Air, which, despite its
beauty, guzzled quarts of oil, then spewed it back into the
air in the form of white smoke—seemed like a trip across

69

the continent in a Conestoga wagon. But the local folk clubs thrived on single acts, and, as usual, their Monday nights were reserved for budding talent. Stand-up comedy felt like an open door. It was possible to assemble a few minutes of material and be onstage *that week,* as opposed to standing in line in some mysterious world in Hollywood, getting no response, no phone calls returned, and no opportunity to perform. On Mondays, I could tour around Orange County, visit three clubs in one night, and be onstage, live, in front of an audience. If I flopped at the Paradox in Tustin, I might succeed an hour later at the Rouge et Noir. I found myself confining the magic to its own segment so I wouldn't be called a magician. Even though the idea of doing comedy had sounded risky when I compared it to the safety of doing trick after trick, I wanted, needed, to be called a comedian. I discovered it was not magic I was interested in but performing in general. Why? Was I in a competition with my father? No, because I wasn't aware of his interest in showbiz until years later. Was my ego out of control and looking for glory? I don't think so; I am fundamentally shy and still feel slightly embarrassed at disproportionate attention. My answer to the question is simple: Who wouldn't want to be in show business?

I looked around the Bird Cage and saw actors who had worked there fifteen years and counting, and I knew it could be a trap for me. With some trepidation, I gave notice. Stormie was gone, Kathy was gone, John Stuart and Paul Shackleton were gone, too, so there were no actual tearful goodbyes. Handshakes with George and Woody. At age twenty-one, three years after I had started at the Bird Cage, I slipped away almost unnoticed.

I CONTINUED TO ATTEND Long Beach State College, taking Stormie-inspired courses in metaphysics, ethics, and logic. New and exhilarating words such as "epistemology," "ontology," "pragmatism," and "existentialism"—words whose definitions alone were stimulating—swirled through my head and reconfigured my thinking. One semester I was taking Philosophy of Language, Continental Rationalism (whatever that is; what, Descartes?), History of Ethics, and to complete the group, Self-Defense, which I found especially humiliating when, one afternoon in class, I was nearly beaten up by a girl wearing boxing gloves. A course in music appreciation focused me on classical music, causing me to miss the pop music of my own era, so I got into the Beatles several years late. I was fixated on studying, and even though I kept my outside jobs, my drive for learning led to a significant improvement from my dismal high school grade average. I was now an A student. I switched to cotton pants called peggers, because I had vowed to grow up and abandon jeans. My look was strictly wholesome Baptist.

A friend lent me some comedy records. There were three by Nichols and May, several by Lenny Bruce, and one by Tom Lehrer, the great song parodist. Mike Nichols and Elaine May recorded without an audience, and I fixated on every nuance. Their comedy was sometimes created by only a subtle vocal shift: "Tell me Dr. Schweitzer, what is this *reverence for life*?" Lenny Bruce, on the records I heard, was doing mostly nonpolitical bits that were hilarious. Warden at a prison riot: "We're giving in to your demands, men! Except the vibrators!" Tom Lehrer influenced me with one bizarre joke: "My brother Henry was a nonconformist. To show you what a nonconformist he was, he spelled his name H-E-N-3-R-Y." Some people fall asleep at night listening to music; I fell asleep to Lenny, Tom, and Mike and Elaine. These albums broke ground and led me to a Darwinian discovery: Comedy could evolve.

On campus I experienced two moments of illumination, both appropriately occurring in the bright sun. Now comfortable with indulging in overthinking, I was walking across the quad when a thought came to me, one that was nearly devastating. To implement the new concept called originality that I had been first introduced to in *Showmanship for Magicians,* and was now presenting itself again in my classes in literature, poetry, and philosophy, I would have to write everything in the act myself. Any line or idea with even a vague feeling of familiarity or provenance had to be expunged. There could be nothing that made the audience feel they weren't seeing something utterly new.

This realization mortified me. I did not know how to write comedy—at all. But I did know I would have to drop some of my best one-liners, all pilfered from gag books and other people's routines, and consequently lose ten minutes from my already strained act. Worse, I would lose another prime gag I had lifted, Carl Ballantine's never-fail Appearing Dove, which had been appropriated by almost every comic magician under the age of twenty. Ballantine would blow up a paper bag and announce that he was going to produce a dove. "Come out flyin'!" he would say. Then he would pop the bag with his hands, and an anemic flutter of feathers would poof out from the sack. The thought of losing all this material was depressing. After several years of working up my weak twenty minutes, I was now starting from almost zero.

I came up with several schemes for developing material. "I laugh in life," I thought, "so why not observe what it is that makes me laugh?" And if I did spot something that was funny, I decided not to just describe it as happening to someone else, but to translate it into the first person, so it was happening *to me*. A guy didn't walk into a bar, I did. I didn't want it to appear that others were nuts; I wanted it to appear that *I* was nuts.

Another method was to idly and abstractedly dream up bits. Sitting in a science class, I stared at the periodic table of the elements that hung behind the professor. That weekend I went onstage at the Ice House and announced, "And now I would like to do a dramatic reading of the periodic table of the elements. Fe ... Au ... He ..." I said. That bit didn't last long.

73

In logic class, I opened my textbook—the last place I was expecting to find comic inspiration—and was startled to find that Lewis Carroll, the supremely witty author of *Alice's Adventures in Wonderland*, was also a logician. He wrote logic textbooks and included argument forms based on the syllogism, normally presented in logic books this way:

All men are mortal.
Socrates is a man.

Therefore, Socrates is mortal.

But Carroll's were more convoluted, and they struck me as funny in a new way:

1) Babies are illogical.
2) Nobody is despised who can manage a crocodile.
3) Illogical persons are despised.

Therefore, babies cannot manage crocodiles.

And:

1) No interesting poems are unpopular among people of real taste.
2) No modern poetry is free from affectation.
3) All your poems are on the subject of soap bubbles.

4) No affected poetry is popular among people of taste.

5) Only a modern poem would be on the subject of soap bubbles.

Therefore, all your poems are uninteresting.

These word games bothered and intrigued me. Appearing to be silly nonsense, on examination they were *absolutely logical*—yet they were still funny. The comedy doors opened wide, and Lewis Carroll's clever fancies from the nineteenth century expanded my notion of what comedy could be. I began closing my show by announcing, "I'm not going home tonight; I'm going to Bananaland, a place where only two things are true, only two things: One, all chairs are green; and two, no chairs are green." Not at Lewis Carroll's level, but the line worked for my contemporaries, and I loved implying that the one thing I believed in was a contradiction.

I also was enamored of the rhythmic poetry of e. e. cummings, and a tantalizing quote from one of his recorded lectures stayed in my head. When asked why he became a poet, he said, "Like the burlesque comedian, I am abnormally fond of that precision which creates movement." The line, with its intriguing reference to comedy, was enigmatic, and it took me ten years to work out its meaning.

The second illuminating moment occurred when I was walking to class from a parking lot so far from campus that I could see the curvature of the earth. Again under the bright California sun, I saw a girl with short black hair, pertly walking in faded blue jeans. I was nervous about saying hello, but she offered me a welcoming smile that said it was okay. She had an unmelodic name—Nina Goldblatt—and she was a professional dancer. We started running into each other accidentally at every opportunity. I only had to get over the hurdle of her dating the handsome actor Vince Edwards, who played the TV doctor Ben Casey, and who was sending limos down to Long Beach to chauffeur her to Hollywood. Somehow I did, and a new romance was on.

Nina was a dancer in *The Mickey Finn Show,* a banjo and pizza whoop-de-do, with an upcoming appearance in Las Vegas on the fabled Strip. I drove five hours to spend the weekend with her and was captivated by the city, but my excitement was dampened by having only four dollars in my pocket. I was so broke that when I hit a nickel slot for fifty cents, it momentarily changed the quality of my life. It was Nina who had the dough, and we learned that Vegas could support even the poorly heeled by offering dollar-twenty-five all-you-can-eat buffets. Nina treated me to some Vegas nightclubs and I fantasized about starring as a lounge act at a spiffy hotel. We went to see the Jets, a two-man comedy-music team whose gags included passing through the audience, using the microphone as a "falsie detector." I enjoyed my time with Nina—she was funny and saucy as well as

76

Nina and me, ca. 1965.

cute—and one year later, she was to have a significant effect on my professional life.

My college roommate, Phil Carey, was an artist and musician. He sang bass, not in a barbershop quartet but for a sophisticated chorale that featured music with complicated rhythms and mismatched twelve-tone arrangements. Phil's contagious enthusiasm got me excited about art, particularly the avant-garde, and we quickly noted that the campus art scene was also a great arena to meet girls. We loved reading magazine reports of New York galleries stuffed with Warhol's Brillo boxes and giant flowers, Lichtenstein's cartoon panels, and throngs of

77

people dressed in black. One afternoon I donned Phil's beret—which meant I was disguised as an artist—and sneaked into his life drawing class, where an attractive nude blonde was casually displaying herself. I was all business on the outside, but on the inside I was shouting, "Yeehaw!" Phil had a developed sense of humor: His cat was named Miles, and when asked if the cat was named after Miles Davis, Phil would say no, it was "and miles to go before I sleep."

Working on a college project, Phil landed an interview with the great American composer Aaron Copland. However, he would have to drive from Los Angeles to Peekskill, New York, to conduct it. I jumped at the chance to go along. In the summer of 1966—I was still twenty and proud that I would make it to New York City before I turned twenty-one—we installed a makeshift cot in the back of my coughing blue windowless VW bus, and we drove across America without stopping. I was trying to write like e. e. cummings, so my correspondence to Nina, all highly romantic, goopy, and filled with references to flowers and stars, read like amateur versions of his poems. Nina saved the letters, but they are too embarrassing to reproduce here.

Three days after we left Los Angeles, Phil and I arrived at Aaron Copland's house, a low-slung A-frame with floor-to-ceiling windows, set in a dappled forest by the road. We knocked on the door, Copland answered it, and over his shoulder we saw a group of men sitting in the living room wearing only skimpy black thongs. He escorted us to his flagstone patio, where I had the demanding job of turning the tape recorder on and off while Phil asked questions about Copland's musical process. We emerged a half hour later with the coveted interview and got in the car, never mentioning the men in skimpy black thongs, because, like trigonometry, we couldn't quite comprehend it. We drove to West Redding, Connecticut, for a tour of the house of another great American composer, the late Charles Ives. Speaking with Ives's son-in-law, George Tyler, we learned the peculiar fact that Ives was an avant-garde composer by night and an insurance agent by day. After a detour to Cambridge, Massachusetts, to cruise the home of my idol cummings, we drove in to glorious Manhattan. Saucer-eyed, we hustled over to the Museum of Modern Art, where we saw, among the Cézannes and Matisses, Dalí's famous painting of melting clocks, the shockingly tiny *The Persistence of Memory*. We were dismayed to find that Warhol and Lichtenstein had not yet been ordained. We drove to Eighth Avenue, and Phil circled the block while I retrieved from the imposing central New York post office a lively and welcome letter from Nina, sent to me care of General Delivery, New York City. I bounded down the massive steps, waving the onionskin envelope aloft for Phil to see, as though it were the lost map of the Incas.

Before we left Cambridge, I sent this postcard to Nina:

Dear Nina,

Today (about an hour ago) I stood in front of e. e. cummings's home at Harvard; his wife is still living there—we saw her. But the most fantastic thing was when we asked directions to Irving Street, the person we asked said to tell Mrs. Cummings hello from the Jameses! She turned out to be William James's great-granddaughter!

Then I added:

I have decided my act is going to go avant-garde. It is the only way to do what I want.

I'm not sure what I meant, but I wanted to use the lingo, and it was seductive to make these pronouncements. Through the years, I have learned there is no harm in charging oneself up with delusions between moments of valid inspiration.

AT THE ICE HOUSE, I had met the comedian George McKelvey. George had an actual career and was quite funny. In reference to radio's invisible crime fighter, the Shadow, he would ask, "If you could be invisible, what would you do? [long pause] Fight crime?" He was in Aspen, Colorado, during spring break, about to work a small folk club, when he broke his leg skiing. Could I fill in for him? he asked. He generously offered me all his salary—I think it was three hundred dollars for the two weeks—which would be more than I had ever earned, anywhere, anytime. I was twenty-one years old in March of 1967 when I headed for the notorious ski resort.

I arrived at a Pan-Abode house—a cedar cabin made from a kit—just outside Aspen. Visiting entertainers were bunked there, and after I made my way through the crunchy snow and stowed my suitcase under my bed, several of us introduced ourselves. One was my co-bill, John McClure, a lanky guitarist with an acute sense of humor. Wandering in later was a pretty waitress named Linda Byers who, I assumed, would fall for me because of my carefully designed, poetry-quoting artist's persona, but who, to my shock, chose John, and they formed a long-term relationship. Also in the house was one of the few English comedians working in America, Jonathan Moore, who played a bagpipe to open his show, scaring the audience with its ancient howl as he entered the club from behind them. Jonathan was older than we were, had been around, wore sunglasses indoors, and had the charm of a well-spoken cynic. His sheepdog, an ecstatic, ball-chasing mop named Winston, dove repeatedly into the deep snowy banks to retrieve our enthusiastically thrown snowballs. Winston didn't seem to mind that they would vanish white on white, and he earnestly pursued the impossible, digging, digging, digging. Jonathan Moore also said something in passing that put my hypochondriacal senses on alert. A local Aspenite had died, and Jonathan offered, "You can't live at this altitude with a bad heart." From then on, whenever I was in Aspen, I had a barely manageable fear that I would suddenly be struck down.

Jonathan's girlfriend Linda Quaderer, Jonathan Moore, Linda Byers, John McClure, Winston, and me.

The nightclub, the Abbey Cellar on Galena Street, was at basement level in the middle of town and hard to find even for us. John and I, in order to drum up business, left little cards on the tables in the upstairs restaurant that read STEVE MARTIN / JOHN MCCLURE, ENTERTAINMENT ORDINAIRE, which to me was hilariously funny, but never seemed to be noticed as a joke.

Aspen was no place for poetry readings, and they were stripped permanently from my act. I was now doing my triptych of banjo playing, comedy, and magic. One evening at the Abbey Cellar, I had my first experience with a serious heckler, who, sitting at the front table with his wife and another straight-looking couple, stood up and said, "See if you think this is funny," and threw a glass of red wine on me. The problem for him was, at this point in the evening, the employees outnumbered the audience. A few seconds later, John McClure and the rough, tough bartender, an Irishman named Mike, appeared like centurions and escorted him out. Eventually, his friends slunk out, too. The expulsion had a downside: The audience was now one third as large and in shock, and remained in stunned silence for the rest of my show. Later, I developed a few defensive lines to use against the

83

unruly: "Oh, I remember when I had my first beer," and if that didn't cool them off, I would use a psychological trick. I would lower my voice and continue with my act, talking almost inaudibly. The audience couldn't hear the show, and they would shut the heckler up on their own.

I was in awe of the red-bearded Mike, who seemed so confident in the divided world of Aspen, where locals with a sense of entitlement were pitted against developers with a sense of condominiums. One evening after closing, I watched him crack open an amyl nitrate, a potent drug for the heart and a dangerous one to fool around with, but rumored to enhance sex. With a long, deep breath, he inhaled its fumes in one nostril, then did the same extended inhale through the other nostril. "Do you want some? It only lasts a few seconds," he said. Not really, but I leaned over and, with the ampoule held far away from my nose, gave it the most tentative sniff possible. My brain exploded. I walked around the club feeling like a colossus with a four-foot-wide lightbulb where my head was supposed to be. Alarmed and anxious, I went sliding into the icy streets, trying to calm down. As for it lasting seconds, I was still vibrating twenty-four hours later. What, I wondered, must Mike feel as he inhaled the freshly broken capsule into both lungs with an effort worthy of the Big Bad Wolf?

The next night I was picked up by a local woman. She was older and looking for sex and, since my boyfriend status with Nina had recently unraveled, I was eager to oblige. Even though I was still reeling from the previous night, we went to her second-floor apartment in a hundred-year-old building and wasted no time. In the middle of this experience, I heard the pop of an amyl nitrate, and then she shoved it toward my nose. I had barely come down from the previous night's blast and I wasn't about to have my head ripped off again. I breathed out and tried to make it appear as though I were breathing in, determined that none of the molecules should get anywhere near me. I was successful but had to act as though I was wowed beyond belief. "Yes, yes!" I lied. After this mess was over, she asked if she could take my picture. I said sure, and she went to get her camera. I moved into her living room, where I casually picked up from her coffee table a wood-bound scrapbook bearing the image of a sleeping Mexican on its cover. Pasted inside were dozens of photos of guys sitting in the chair I was now occupying.

My experience at the Abbey Cellar was important to me, but not as important as what was going on after hours. John and I shared a room, and his future partner, Linda, would join us for lengthy chats. What we discussed was the new zeitgeist. I don't know how it got to this bedroom in Aspen, but it was creeping everywhere simultaneously. I didn't yet know its name but found out later it was called Flower Power, and I was excited to learn that we were now living in the Age of Aquarius, an age when, at least astrologically, the world would be taken over by macramé. Anticorporate, individual, and freak-based, it

85

proposed that all we had to do was love each other and there would be no more wars or strife. Nothing could have been newer or more appealing. The vast numbers of us who changed our thoughts and lives for this belief proved that, yes, it is possible to fool all of the people some of the time. The word "love" was being tossed around as though only we insiders knew its definition. But any new social philosophy is good for creativity. New music was springing up, new graphics twisted and swirled as if on LSD, and an older generation was being glacially inched aside to make room for the freshly weaned new one. The art world, always contrarian, responded to psychedelia with monochrome and minimalism. It was fun trying to "turn" a young conservative, which was easy because our music was better. I remember trying to convince a member of the Dallas Ski Club that "Yummy, Yummy, Yummy (I've Got Love in My Tummy)" was not really a good song no matter how much he liked it. After two weeks in Aspen, I went back to Los Angeles feeling like an anointed prophet, taking my friends aside and burping out the new philosophy.

I CONTINUED TO PURSUE my studies and half believed I might try for a doctorate in philosophy and become a teacher, as teaching is, after all, a form of show business. I'm not sure what the purpose of fooling myself was, but I toyed with the idea for several semesters. I concluded that not to continue with comedy would place a question in my mind that would nag me for the rest of my life: Could I have had a career in performing? Everything was dragging me toward the arts; even the study of modern philosophy suggested that philosophy was nonsense. A classmate, Ron Barnett, and I spent hours engaged in late-night mind-altering dialogues in Laundromats and parking lots, discussing Ludwig Wittgenstein, the great Austrian semanticist. Wittgenstein's investigations disallowed so many types of philosophical discussions that we were convinced the very discussion we were having was impossible. Soon I felt that a career in the irrational world of creativity not only made sense but had moral purpose.

I was living several lives at once: I was a student at Long Beach State; I sometimes filled in at the Bird Cage Theatre; and at night I performed in various folk clubs with an eclectic, homemade comedy act that wasn't to reach its flash point for another decade. One of the clubs I played was Ledbetter's, a comparatively classy beer-and-wine nightspot a few blocks from UCLA that catered to the college crowd. I was taken under the wing of its owner, Randy Sparks, a theatrical entrepreneur who had founded the New Christy Minstrels, a highly successful folk act. I opened the show for his new acts, the Back Porch Majority and the New Society, two massive, stage-filling folk groups who offered wholesome high spirits and some pretty funny comedy to the Westwood Village audiences. Fats Johnson, a jovial folksinger who dressed to kill in black

87

suits with white ruffled shirts and wore elaborate rings on his guitar-strumming hand, often headlined the club. When I asked him about his philosophy of dressing for the stage, he said firmly, "Always look better than they do."

Now that most of my work was in Westwood, Long Beach State College, forty miles away, seemed like Siberia. I transferred to my third college, UCLA, so I could be closer to the action, and I took several courses there. One was an acting class, the kind that feels like prison camp and treats students like detainees who need to be broken; another was a course in television writing, which seemed practical. I also continued my studies in philosophy. I had done pretty well in symbolic logic at Long Beach, so I signed up for Advanced Symbolic Logic at my new school. Saying that I was studying Advanced Symbolic Logic at UCLA had a nice ring; what had been nerdy in high school now had mystique. However, I went to class the first day and discovered that UCLA used a different set of symbols from those I had learned at Long Beach. To catch up, I added a class in Logic 101, which meant I was studying beginning logic and advanced logic at the same time. I was overwhelmed, and shocked to find that I couldn't keep up. I had reached my math limit as well as my philosophy limit. I abruptly changed my major to theater and, free from the workload of my logic classes, took a relaxing inhale of crisp California air. But on the exhale, I realized that I was now investing in no other future but show business.

The physical distance from each other had permanently

broken up Nina and me, and she had left school to pursue her dancing career. But overnight, there were dozens of new people in my life. Pot smoking was de rigueur—this being the sixties—and since I was now a regular at Ledbetter's, I was living rent-free over the garage of a mansion in the exclusive area of Bel Air, thanks to the generosity of Randy Sparks and his wife, Diane. Even though I was armed with only a comedy act that was at best hit-and-miss, I was fearless and ready to go. Among the crowd of singers and musicians whose local fame I assumed was worldwide was a sylph-like figure, a nonsinger and nonmusician who nonetheless seemed to be regarded quite highly in this small showbiz matrix. Her name was Melissa, but her friends called her Mitzi. She was twenty years old, with a Katharine Hepburn beauty and a similarly willowy frame. She was intelligent, energetic, and lit from inside. Her hair was ash brown, and always at the end of one of her long and slender arms was a Nikon camera with a lens the size of a can of Campbell's soup.

When her current romance withered, Mitzi and I became entwined. After several weeks of courtship, I was ready for family inspection and she invited me to her parents' house for dinner. Mitzi's last name was Trumbo. Her father was screenwriter Dalton Trumbo, one of the notorious Hollywood Ten, a group of writers and directors who were blacklisted during the Red Scare of the early fifties. During his congressional hearing,

Trumbo vociferously challenged the right of his inquisitors to interrogate him, prompting a frustrated committee member to scream, "You are out of order, sir! You are out of order!" in a futile attempt to get him to shut up. It

Mitzi Trumbo, 1965.

was Trumbo who wrote the screenplays for *Spartacus, Lonely Are the Brave, Hawaii, Exodus,* and *Papillon;* whose personal letters read like Swiftian essays; who had to flee to Mexico for several years and write under pseudonyms such as Sam Jackson and James Bonham in order to escape McCarthyism; and whom, at this stage in my tunnel-visioned life, I had never heard of. Mitzi later told me that there were no wrong numbers in their household because any unknown name the caller asked for was assumed to be one of Trumbo's aliases.

90
—

From my perspective, Mitzi was a sophisticate. She had traveled. She was politically aware and had attended Reed College in Oregon, a bastion of liberal thought. Her intelligence was informed by her family history. When I went to dinner at her home in the Hollywood Hills, I did not know that the few months I would spend in this family's graces would broaden my life.

My first glimpse of Dalton Trumbo revealed an engrossed intellect—not finessing his latest screenplay but sorting the seeds and stems from a brick of pot. "Pop smokes marijuana," Mitzi explained, "with the wishful thought of cutting down on his drinking." Sometimes, from their balcony, I would see Trumbo walking laps around the perimeter of the pool. He held a small counter in one hand and clicked it every time he passed the diving board. These health walks were compromised by the cigarette he constantly held in his other hand.

Dalton Trumbo was the first raconteur I ever met. The family dinners—frequented by art dealers, actors, and artists of all kinds, including the screenwriters Hugo Butler and Ring Lardner, Jr., and the director George Roy Hill—were lively, political, and funny. I had never been in a house where conversations were held during dinner or where food was placed before me after being prepared behind closed doors. It was also the first time I ever heard swear words spoken by adults in front of their offspring. Lyndon Johnson's Vietnam bombing policy dominated the conversation, and the government's ironfisted response to war protesters rankled the dinner guests, since the Hollywood Ten were long familiar with oppression. Trumbo had a patriarchal delivery whether he was on a rant or discussing art or slinging wit, but nothing he said was elitist—though I do remember him saying, as he spread his arms to indicate the china and silver serving ladles, "Admittedly, we do live well."

Trumbo's wife, Cleo, beautiful like Mitzi, was at the head of the table when Trumbo was downstairs writing. Cleo was the person actually in charge and could not have been more welcoming. She extended an open dinner invitation to Mitzi and me, and as I was deeply broke, we always accepted. The food was delicious and the company spectacular, so we did not regret missing out on the "health salads" served at our local incense-burning restaurants—gunky concoctions of cheese-laden, ham-draped iceberg lettuce doused with creamy dressing.

One evening after dinner, we adjourned to the living room—something else I had never done before—and I was surprised to see a marijuana cigarette passed among the guests. The joint finally got to Trumbo, and he clasped it between his knuckles like a German officer in a movie. He didn't pass it along, just held it and puffed on it but did not inhale. With a broad grin, Mitzi leaned over to me and said, "Pop doesn't know how to smoke pot. He thinks you smoke it like a cigar, and he never gets high."

The family's liberal bent was never fully tested. When I asked Mitzi if her parents knew about my slipping in the garden door of her bedroom late at night and leaving at daybreak, she said that Cleo knew but Pop would not be pleased. Hence, in the early mornings, I started my car gingerly, thinking that if I turned the key slowly, the engine would not make so much noise.

The Trumbo house was modern, built on a hillside, and extended down three floors into a ravine. The walls in the living room were large, and they give me my most vivid memory of the house, for they were covered with art. Political art. I had never seen real paintings in a

Dancing with Mitzi
in front of the Hiram Williams painting.

house, and this might have been where my own inclination toward owning pictures began. In the entry was an eight-foot-high Baconesque painting by Hiram Williams, a picture of several businessmen, their hands bloody, emerging from a white background. In the dining room was a William Gropper, depicting members of the House Un-American Activities Committee grotesquely outlined in fluorescent green against a murky background. There was a Raphael Soyer, a Moses Soyer, and a Jack Levine painting of Hindenburg making Hitler chancellor. These

Steve Martin
a fantastically
clever comedian, magician and
all-around good guy

An ad for the Ice House; photo by Mitzi Trumbo.

artists are obscure today but not forgotten. Gropper's art depicted politicos as porcine bullies, and Jack Levine's well-brushed social realism had a biting edge and fit the politics of the family perfectly.

Mitzi became my official photographer, and she snapped dozens of rolls of film, all to find the perfect publicity photo. It being the sixties, there were many shots of me with a flower on my head or a daisy between my teeth. We spent one morning taking photos in Fern Dell, where a stream flowed down the concrete center of a man-made mini–tropical rain forest set in the heart of Los Angeles, which up to that point was the most lush place I had ever seen. Later that day, we attended an anti–Vietnam War protest where I was lucky to get—then unlucky enough to lose—my draft card autographed by Cassius Clay, soon to be the most famous person in the world, Muhammad Ali.

The war was rapidly consuming young men, and the draft was closing in. The thought of being shipped off to Vietnam for possible dismemberment scared me, especially after I read Dalton Trumbo's antiwar book, *Johnny Got His Gun*, the story of a young soldier who wakes to discover he has lost his legs, arms, mouth, nose, eyes, and ears and is left with only the ability to think. In the face of this war, which snared so many, I had a case of rolling luck. First I was exempt because I was in college. When the college deferment lifted, I became 1-Y, unacceptable because of migraine headaches, which I had

95

exaggerated. When the definition of 1-Y was tightened and I was moved up to 1-A, the draft went to a lottery, and I drew a middling number. As my number approached, the army went to all-volunteer, and I was saved from an alternate life. But I cannot end this story without a solemn bow to those who weren't so fortunate.

I got a one-show job performing near the Russian River in Northern California. I drove there in my second great car, a yellow 1966 Ford Mustang (my third and last great car was a yellow 1967 Jaguar XK-E. Then I lost all interest in cars). Up north, I reconnoitered with Mitzi, and she took photos of me canoeing. Unfortunately, she didn't photograph the job I had, performing at a drive-in theater at three P.M. under the afternoon sun while a dozen cars hooked up to the sound system listened through window speakers. If the drive-in patrons thought a joke was funny, they honked. You might think I'm exaggerating, but I'm not.

Once, on the way to the Trumbo house, Mitzi warned me, "Pop's in a bad mood today. He's got a screenplay due in four days and he hasn't started it yet." The screenplay was for the movie *The Fixer*, starring Alan Bates. Eventually, the work got done and the movie was ready to shoot. Trumbo encouraged Mitzi to join him and she was whisked off to Budapest for the duration of the film. After I'd received several charming letters from her and then noticed a lag in the regularity of their arrival, Mitzi sent me a gentle and direct Dear John letter. She had been

96

swept away by the director John Frankenheimer, who, twenty years later, tried and failed to seduce my then wife, the actress Victoria Tennant, whom he was directing in a movie. Mitzi was simply too alluring to be left alone in a foreign country, and I was too hormonal to be left alone in Hollywood. Incidentally, Frankenheimer died a few years ago, but it was not I who killed him.

Television

I WAS STILL TWENTY-ONE when I was politely booted from Randy and Diane Sparks's garage apartment. I moved to an unincorporated area called Palms, adjacent to the historic MGM Studios, and shared a small guesthouse with the sharp, deadpan comedian Gary Mule Deer ("I think we should put pictures of missing transvestites on cartons of half-and-half") and the lonely-voiced singer-guitarist Michael Johnson. I continued to work at Ledbetter's and attend classes at UCLA. But while I studied halfheartedly in Westwood, Nina had entered the world of real show business. She had changed her name to the more mellifluous Nina Lawrence and landed a job dancing on *The Smothers Brothers Comedy Hour*, the hippest

99

thing on television and Flower-Powered all over the place. She had begun dating Mason Williams, the head writer on the show. I still had an affectionate crush on her and was glad for her and sick all at the same time. Mason Williams, exuberant, infused with creativity, and the future composer of the smash hit "Classical Gas," drove an elegant 1938 Pierce-Arrow and could talk the new aesthetic—essentially, the appreciation for all things quirky and creative—much better than I could. Where I could only recite poetry, Mason actually was a poet. He lived in a rented house in the Hollywood Hills with spar-kling views of Los Angeles out the bedroom's vast picture window. I imagined Mason and Nina doing it every which-a-way for anyone with a pair of binoculars to see. But these days, who could mind? We weren't a couple anymore, and Free Love, man, Free Love! Which, by the way, was the single greatest concept a young man has ever heard. This was a time when intercourse, or some version of it, was a way of saying hello. About three years later, women got wise and my frustration returned to normal levels.

I was almost but not quite in a financial bind when Nina phoned me to say that the Smothers Brothers— exercising the slogan of the day, "Never Trust Anyone over Thirty"—wanted to experiment and hire a few young writers for their hit TV show. In college, influ-enced by Jack Douglas's book *My Brother Was an Only Child* and Mason Williams's *The Mason Williams Reading*

Matter, I had composed, as a defiant alternative to coherent essay writing, some goofy one-paragraph stories with such titles as "The Day the Dopes Came Over," "What to Say When the Ducks Show Up," and "Cruel Shoes." Nina told me to send over my stories. I did, and she gave them to Mason.

The collection of scraps I sent was sketchy, half-baked material that I never would have submitted to a college English class for fear of expulsion. But Mason liked it, or maybe he just liked Nina, and having never written anything professionally in my life, I was hired as a tryout for the few remaining weeks of the *Smothers* season. I gingerly went to my television writing instructor at UCLA and told him I had to resign from the class—and school—because I had gotten a job writing for television. Years later, I learned that because my material had not made it past the final judges at the top, Mason, in an act of artistic generosity, had paid this newcomer out of his own pocket.

My professional writing career started off painfully. The older writers were rightfully suspicious of this kid, especially since my only qualification was being under thirty, and I felt the pressure to deliver. I was timid and unsure of myself in this suddenly wider world. If I was asked to write an intro for the folksinger Judy Collins, I would write, "And now, ladies and gentlemen, here's folksinger Judy Collins!" One afternoon I was in the studio, watching a rehearsal of a sketch dealing with television.

Tommy Smothers came up to me and said directly, "We need an intro for this bit. Can you write it?" This question was put to me with a clear implication that my job was on the line. I said yes but meant no. I went upstairs to my office as if I were on a march to the gallows; my mind was blank. Blanker than blank. I was a tabula rasa. I put paper in the typewriter and impotently stared at it. Finally, a great line occurred to me, except it belonged to my roommate, the comedian Gary Mule Deer. But it was perfect for this intro, so why not call him and ask if I could use it? By a miracle, he was home. I explained that I was stuck. He said sure, use it. I went downstairs, handed in the line, and Dick Smothers read the joke: "It has been proven that more Americans watch television than any other appliance." Two highly experienced writers, Hal Goodman and Al Goldman, with credits extending back to Jack Benny, came up to me and said, "Did you write that joke?" "Yes," I said. "Good work," they said. If, at that moment, I had been hooked up to a lie detector, it would have spewed smoke. The event must have been cathartic, because afterward, I relaxed and was able to contribute fully to the show.

The season ended, and I was asked to work on a summer replacement show, the malappropriately titled *The Summer Brothers Smothers Show*, starring Glen Campbell. Glen was a former studio musician who had just risen to stardom with his first big hit, John Hartford's "Gentle on My Mind." I was twenty-two years old when I found myself standing in a small room at CBS on Fairfax with a few other writers, including John Hartford, while Pete Seeger strummed his banjo not five feet from me. Around the calfskin head of Pete's banjo was written in ink, THIS MACHINE SURROUNDS HATE AND FORCES IT TO SURRENDER (an allusion to Woody Guthrie's earlier guitar slogan, THIS MACHINE KILLS FASCISTS). We pitched concepts for Pete's appearance, but his idea was the best. He would sing "Waist Deep in the Big Muddy (and the Big Fool Says to Push On)" over images of the increasingly tragic war in Vietnam. Glen Campbell probably hadn't known what he was getting into, but he endorsed us all the way.

I was teamed with the hilarious Bob Einstein—an advertising writer who had found his way to CBS—and fortunately, as we shared a windowless office and worked together fourteen hours a day, we became inseparable friends. Bob and I were perfect writing foils. We had a mutual regard for Laurel and Hardy, Jerry Lewis, Daffy Duck, and Mel Blanc's peculiar genius, and we could make each other laugh until we were breathless. If I accidentally banged my head on a stage pipe, Bob would collapse in hysterics and, following his lead, so would I. At least eight of our fourteen working hours were spent laughing until we were in pain, then trying to decide if what we were laughing at was usable or just comic delirium. Bob later achieved fame as Super Dave, a bumbling TV daredevil.

Though Bob and I were a team, I sometimes worked

with another young writer/performer, Rob Reiner, later to make his mark as the director of, among other films, *When Harry Met Sally* and the classic *This Is Spinal Tap*. Rob, in a coincidence that was yet to happen, was the son of my future film director, Carl Reiner. Rob and I closed our first season with a strong finish. We wrote a ten-minute finale combining short sketches with classic rock songs from the fifties. At that time "oldies but goodies" was a new concept. The segment was a hit and Rob and I gave ourselves credit, whether it was accurate or not, for starting a fifties music revival. We wrote it for Glen Campbell and Bobbie Gentry (who was still riding on the success of "Ode to Billy Joe"), and when Bobbie appeared onstage in an "itsy-bitsy teeny-weeny yellow polka-dot bikini," all the writers' jaws dropped. We hadn't known she'd started as a chorus girl in Las Vegas.

I had a short-lived but troublesome worry. What if writing comedy was a dead end because one day everything would have been done and we writers would just run out of stuff? I assuaged myself with my own homegrown homily: Comedy is a distortion of what is happening, and there will always be something happening. This problem solved, I grew more confident as a writer and slid into steady work the following season, thanks to an endorsement from Bob Einstein, on *The Smothers Brothers Comedy Hour*. I even had a few walk-on appearances where I inevitably played "the hippie." The satirical show had taken a big left turn, which suited my politics perfectly. Constantly making news because of CBS's censorship policy, *The Smothers Brothers Comedy Hour* was the only source on prime-time television for both satire and contemporary music acts such as the Doors and the Beatles.

Bob Einstein, Nina Lawrence, Don Wyatt, and me, in costume for a *Smothers* sketch.

Though the new writing job frequently required all-nighters, I continued to service my stand-up career. I would bomb regularly at the Ice House, but the audiences were so sparse that the proprietor, Bob Stane, couldn't tell if I was flopping or the house was too empty. One night I realized I had been on for twenty minutes and had not gotten a single laugh from the dead Tuesday-night crowd. I thought, "Why not go for the record?" I set my mind to it and finished the show without having roused one

105

snicker. However, there was a sign of encouragement from these early jobs, and years later I heard it phrased perfectly by Bill Cosby. He said that early in his career, when the audience wasn't laughing, he could hear the waitresses laughing, and they saw the show night after night. I noticed that the waitresses were laughing.

MY LIFE HAD BEEN ALTERNATELY inching or leaping upward: I was proud of my job on the Smothers Brothers' show. I had some cash. My sex life was abundant and selfish. Things were rolling along nicely when I experienced a crushing psychological surprise. One night I was off to the movies with my friends John McClure, George McKelvey, and his wife, Carole. We were going to see Mel Brooks's *The Producers*, and we decided to smoke a little pot, which had become a dietary staple for me. So now I was high. In the car on the way to the theater, I felt my mind being torn from its present location and lifted into the ether. My discomfort intensified, and I experienced an eerie distancing from my own self that crystallized into morbid doom. I mutely waited for the feeling to pass. It didn't, and I finally said, "I feel strange." We got out of the car, and John, George, and Carole walked me along Sunset Boulevard in the night. I decided to go into the theater, thinking it might be distracting. During the film, I sat in stoic silence as my heart began to race above two hundred beats per minute and the saliva drained from my mouth so completely that I could not move my tongue. I assumed this was the heart attack I had been waiting for, though I wasn't feeling pain. I was, however, experiencing extreme fear; I thought I was dying, and I can't explain to you why I just sat there. After the movie, I considered checking myself in to a hospital. But if I went to the hospital, I would miss work the next day, which might make me expendable at CBS, where my career was just launching. My friends walked me along Sunset again, and I remember humming, "Whenever I feel afraid, I hold my head erect and whistle a happy tune" from *The King and I*. I spent the night on George and Carole's couch in absolute terror. I kept wondering, "Am I dying?" but was more concerned with the question "Do I have to quit my job?"

I survived the night and struggled in to work the next morning. I was not relieved, but I was calmer; I confessed to Bob Einstein what had happened and found that as soon as I discussed the symptoms, they arose again with full intensity. However, I somehow maintained my implacable façade.

The cycle was unbreakable. Any relief was followed by the worry of recurrence, which itself provoked the symptoms. After a few weeks, a list of triggers developed. I couldn't go back into a movie theater, and I didn't for at least ten years. I never smoked pot again, or got involved in the era's preoccupation with illicit substances (I'm sure this event helped me avoid the scourge of cocaine).

However, the worst trigger was a certain event that, cruelly, happened every day. It was *night*. Eventually, I could find my way through the daytime, but as I left work, winding my way up the canyon streets as the sun set, I imagined feeling the slight rise in elevation and the air getting thinner. Nuts, I know. As a teenager, I had mixed a somber home life with a jubilant life away from the house. Now I could be funny, alert, and involved while nursing internal chaos, believing that death was inching nearer with each eroding episode of terror. I learned over the next months that I could do several things at once: be a comedy writer, be a stand-up comedian, and endure private mortal fear. Thankfully, after a difficult year, my specific dread of nightfall faded. I suppose I was too practical to have such an inconvenient phobia.

I discovered there was a name for what was happening to me. Reading medical and psychology books, I found my symptoms exactly described and named as an anxiety attack. I felt a sense of relief from the simple understanding that I was not alone. I read that these panic attacks were not dangerous, just gravely unpleasant. The symptoms were comparable to the biological changes the body experiences when put in danger, as if you were standing in front of an object of fear, such as an unleashed lion. In an anxiety attack you have all the symptoms of fear, yet there is no lion. I could not let self-doubt or lack of talent cause me to fail at this new writing job—this lion—which was the gateway to my next life as an entertainer. I carefully buried this fear; I was in over my head, but my conscious mind wouldn't allow that thought to exist, and my body rebelled that night at the movie theater. At least this is my ten-cent diagnosis. I continued to suffer the attacks while I went on with my work, refusing to let this inner nightmare affect my performing or writing career. Though panic attacks are gone from my life now—they receded as slowly as the ice around Greenland—they were woven throughout two decades of my life. When I think of the moments of elation I have experienced over some of my successes, I am astounded at the number of times they have been accompanied by elation's hellish opposite.

IN THE LATE SIXTIES, comedy was in transition. The older school told jokes and stories, punctuated with the drummer's rim shot. Of the new school, Bill Cosby—one of the first to tell stories you actually believed were true—and Bob Newhart—who startled everyone with innovative, low-key delivery and original material—had achieved icon status. Mort Sahl tweaked both sides of the political fence with his college-prof delivery, but soon the audiences were too stoned to follow his coherent sentences. George Carlin and Richard Pryor, though very funny, were still a few years away from their final artistic breakthroughs. Lenny Bruce had died several years earlier, fighting both the system and drugs, and his work was already in revival because of his caustic brilliance that made authority nervous. Vietnam, the first televised war, split the country, and one's left or right bent could be recognized by haircuts and clothes. The country was angry, and so was comedy, which was addressed to insiders. Cheech and Chong spoke to the expanding underground by rolling the world's largest doobie on film. There were exceptions: Don Rickles seemed to glide over the generation gap with killer appearances on *The Tonight Show*, and Johnny Carson remained a gentle satirist while maintaining a nice glossary of naughty-boy breast jokes. Tim Conway and Harvey Korman, two great comic sketch actors working for the affable genius Carol Burnett, were deeply funny. The television free-for-all called *Laugh-In* kept its sense of joy, thanks in part to Goldie Hawn's unabashed goofiness and producer George Schlatter's perceptive use of her screwups, but even that show had high political content. In general, however, a comedian in shackles for indecent language, or a singer's arrest for obscene gestures, thrilled the growing underground audience. Silliness was just not appropriate for hip culture. It was this circumstance that set the stage for my success eight years later.

IN A COLLEGE PSYCHOLOGY CLASS, I had read a treatise on comedy explaining that a laugh was formed when the storyteller created tension, then, with the punch line, released it. I didn't quite get this concept, nor do I still, but it stayed with me and eventually sparked my second wave of insights. With conventional joke telling, there's a moment when the comedian delivers the punch line, and the audience knows it's the punch line, and their response ranges from polite to uproarious. What bothered me about this formula was the nature of the laugh it inspired, a vocal acknowledgment that a joke had been told, like automatic applause at the end of a song.

A skillful comedian could coax a laugh with tiny indicators such as a vocal tic (Bob Hope's "But I wanna tell ya") or even a slight body shift. Jack E. Leonard used to punctuate jokes by slapping his stomach with his hand. One night, watching him on *The Tonight Show,* I noticed that several of his punch lines had been unintelligible, and the audience had actually laughed at nothing but the cue of his hand slap.

These notions stayed with me for months, until they formed an idea that revolutionized my comic direction: What if there were no punch lines? What if there were no indicators? What if I created tension and never released it? What if I headed for a climax, but all I delivered was an anticlimax? What would the audience do with all that tension? Theoretically, it would have to come out sometime. But if I kept denying them the formality of a punch line, the audience would eventually pick their own place to laugh, essentially out of desperation. This type of laugh seemed stronger to me, as they would be laughing at something *they chose,* rather than being told exactly when to laugh.

111

To test my idea, at my next appearance at the Ice House, I went onstage and began: "I'd like to open up with sort of a 'funny comedy bit.' This has really been a big one for me . . . it's the one that put me where I am today. I'm sure most of you will recognize the title when I mention it; it's the Nose on Microphone routine [pause for imagined applause]. And it's always funny, no matter how many times you see it."

I leaned in and placed my nose on the mike for a few long seconds. Then I stopped and took several bows, saying, "Thank you very much." "That's it?" they thought. Yes, that was it. The laugh came not then, but only after they realized I had already moved on to the next bit.

Now that I had assigned myself to an act without jokes, I gave myself a rule. Never let them know I was bombing: *This is funny, you just haven't gotten it yet.* If I wasn't offering punch lines, I'd never be standing there with egg on my face. It was essential that I never show doubt about what I was doing. I would move through my act without pausing for the laugh, as though everything were an aside. Eventually, I thought, the laughs would be playing catch-up to what I was doing. Everything would be either delivered in passing, or the opposite, an elaborate presentation that climaxed in pointlessness. Another rule was to make the audience believe that I thought I was fantastic, that my confidence could not be shattered. They had to believe that I didn't care if they laughed at all, and that this act was going on with or without them.

I was having trouble ending my show. I thought, "Why not make a virtue of it?" I started closing with extended bowing, as though I heard heavy applause. I kept insisting that I needed to "beg off." *No, nothing, not even this ovation I am imagining, can make me stay.* My goal was to make the audience laugh but leave them unable to describe what it was that had made them laugh. In other words, like the helpless state of giddiness experienced by close friends tuned in to each other's sense of humor, *you had to be there.*

At least that was the theory. And for the next eight years, I rolled it up a hill like Sisyphus.

My first reviews came in. One said, "This so-called 'comedian' should be told that jokes are supposed to have punch lines." Another said I represented "the most serious booking error in the history of Los Angeles music."

"Wait," I thought, "let me explain my theory!"

MY JOB WITH THE SMOTHERS BROTHERS allowed me to move to the hippie center of Southern California, Laurel Canyon. In 1968 Laurel Canyon was considered by the in crowd to be a nature reserve because of the presence of trees, even though the democratic Los Angeles smog covered all areas. Joni Mitchell lived there, so did Carole King, so did Kenny Loggins and Frank Zappa. I never met any of them, but I did reconnect with the person who, for the next fifteen years, would be the most

113

significant figure in my performing life. His name was Bill McEuen, and he was the older brother of my high school friend John McEuen. John, a musician since the ninth grade, had joined a group, the Nitty Gritty Dirt Band, and Bill, who aspired to be a showbiz entrepreneur in the mold of Elvis's Colonel Parker, was managing them. It was simply coincidence that Bill and I had both moved, with intermittent stops, from Garden Grove to Laurel Canyon.

Bill had a deep love of early blues, country, and bluegrass music. He would pick up his guitar and sing Jimmie Rodgers's line, "He's in the jailhouse now!" and

In my Laurel Canyon apartment. Notice the Ed Kienholz on the wall, one of the first artworks I ever bought, acquired from a local gallery.

snap a string, giving the note a slight percussion. He also spotted genius. At Pepe's, a dinky club in St. Louis, he saw an act called the Allman Joys and brought them to Hollywood. They changed their name to Hour Glass, and he represented them for a while before they became the Allman Brothers Band. A few years later, he would create and produce a revered country music album, *Will the Circle Be Unbroken,* for which, it seems to me, everyone gets credit but him, even though Bill dreamed it all up and made it happen. He corralled some recording time for me at those Nashville sessions—after Mother Maybelle Carter, Doc Watson, Earl Scruggs, and Jimmy Martin had gone home for the evening—to lay down some banjo tunes I had written. In 1981 the songs appeared on my final last-gasp comedy album, *The Steve Martin Brothers.*

Bill McEuen was rebellious, defiant, and loved to watch the big guy squirm. After I had achieved success, he said to me, "Right now there are a lot of old-time comedians saying, 'What the fuck?'" He had banged his way out of nowhere, too, living just a few miles from me in Garden Grove and growing up under the thumb of a critical father. He had long hair before it was fashionable and kept it not only after it was unfashionable but forever. He also loved comedy. We were united in our worship of Johnny Carson, Don Rickles, Steve Allen, and Jerry Lewis. You can hear Bill's laugh buried somewhere on each of my albums. He even came up with one of my staple jokes of the period: "Do you mind if I smoke? Uh, no, do you mind if I fart?"

We started hanging around together—breakfast, lunch, and dinner—along with his beautiful wife, Alice, who was an excellent photographer. My MGB GT seated two, which meant one of us had to ride in the hatchback trunk, and it was always Bill, who, at six-four, had to curl up like a cat to fit into the car. Bill, after seeing my act a hundred times, asked if he could manage me. "What's a manager?" I said. After he explained, I didn't quite understand, and I don't think he did, either, but we struck a handshake deal for no other reason than that we had nothing to lose.

Bill and Alice McEuen, me, and their cat "White Cat," in Laurel Canyon.

STEVE MARTIN

John McEuen, whom I hadn't seen in about a year, came to the house. He had been on the road and grown his hair long, which surprised me, because I was still resisting. He noted my response, stroked his locks, and said, "Part of the business." Soon after, I grew my hair long and with my earnings from *The Smothers Brothers Comedy Hour,* financed a garish collection of turquoise jewelry that I would wear onstage. I was now a full-blown hippie, though not walking around stoned because of my earlier disastrous experience. I riffed on the drug era with this bit, which was delivered in a secretive, low whisper:

"I'm on drugs. . . . You know what I'm talking about. . . . I like to get small. . . . It's very dangerous for kids, because they get realllly small. . . . I know I shouldn't get small when I'm driving, but I was drivin' around the other day and a cop pulls me over . . . says, 'Hey, are you small?' I say, 'No, I'm tall, I'm tall!' He says, 'I'm gonna have to measure you.' They give you a little test with a balloon. If you can get inside it, they know you're small . . . and they can't put you in a regular cell, either, 'cause you walk right out."

The Smothers Brothers show continued to rankle the brass at both CBS and the federal halls of power. Sketches dealing with race, war, and politics, mixed in with anomalies such as Kate Smith singing "God Bless America," made it a hit in the ratings and at the watercooler. It thrived on controversy, but we writers didn't know the

No comment.

level of rancor the Brothers were facing. One morning in 1969, I was driving to work when I heard on the radio that the Smothers Brothers show had been ignominiously axed. Ostensibly, CBS canceled the show because of late delivery of an episode, but I knew what really had canceled it: a trickle-down from President Nixon. The Brothers had surely made Nixon's enemies list, and probably all of us writers had, too, and the political pressure must have been too much for lumbering CBS, which didn't need static from the FCC. After the show's demise, our team of eight writers won Emmys, the academy's defiant response to the CBS brass. Even after this gold-plated recognition, my father still urged me to go back to college so I would "have something to fall back on."

Comedy was now fully charged with political energy. George Carlin transformed himself from the Hippy Dippy Weatherman into a true social commentator. So did the volatile Richard Pryor, who dropped the gags, appealed to the underground audience, and used "motherfucker" as poetic punctuation. Robert Klein was the educated one; you sat in the audience nodding in agreement with his tart observations. After *The Smothers Brothers Comedy Hour* fell, I joined in with my never-miss Nixon jokes ("Nixon's best friend is Bebe Rebozo, a name that means 'to have bozo-ed again'"). All I had to do was mention Nixon's name, and there were laughs from my collegiate audiences.

Bob Einstein and I had become a solid workhorse writing team. When *The Smothers Brothers* ended, we continued to get jobs, including *The Sonny & Cher Comedy Hour*, which kept me busy for seven months out of the year. During the hiatuses, I would slog away at my act. Bill had put me on the road, opening the show for the Nitty Gritty Dirt Band, and I am grateful to them because they really didn't need me. We went everywhere. Atlanta, Spokane, Madison, Little Rock, Tallahassee, you name it, I was there. Colleges, clubs, and concert halls in what seemed like every state in the union. One magical night, on a lonely road in upstate New York, the bus pulled over and we all got out for a stretch of the legs. We looked north into the moonless black sky. Above us, in this low latitude, shimmered the aurora borealis.

Mostly, I was alone on these road trips, and I would while away the solitary daytime hours by indulging my growing interest in American art of the nineteenth and twentieth centuries. I haunted museums and galleries, making quick visual checks in the local antique stores in hopes of finding a Winslow Homer that had gone astray. I never did, but I managed to buy a nineteenth-century picture by the English artist John Everett Millais, thinking I had made the find of the century, only to discover that it was a tired old fake that had been around the art market for years. This was a cheap lesson in my art-collecting hobby, which would develop fully a decade later. I also killed time in college libraries, browsing for books on American art. After spotting a rare and valuable book in the stacks at the University of Tulsa—it was Mabel Dodge Luhan's early treatise on southwestern painting, *Taos and Its Artists*—I wondered if I could smuggle it past the low-tech librarian. But my better judgment prevailed, and I left it in place.

IN LOS ANGELES, there was an exploding number of new afternoon television talk shows. *The Della Reese Show,*

The Merv Griffin Show, The Virginia Graham Show, The Dinah Shore Show, The Mike Douglas Show, and my favorite, *The Steve Allen Show.* Steve Allen had a vibrant comedy spirit, and if you tuned in, you might catch him playing Ping-Pong while suspended from a crane a hundred feet in the air, or becoming a human tea bag by dropping himself in a tank of water filled with lemons. In his standard warm-up for the studio audience, when he was asked, "Do they get this show in Omaha?" Steve would answer, "They see it, but they don't get it."

I had developed a small reputation from my appearances at the Ice House, and on May 6, 1969, I wrangled a meeting and auditioned in an office for Steve Allen's two producers, Elias Davis and David Pollock. They accepted me with more ease than I expected, and when I spoke with them afterward, they commented, "There seems to be a dearth of young comedians right now." I looked puzzled. I said, "That's odd, I don't think there are many at all." Their stares made me realize my blunder. I knew the word, but I had the definition backward.

For my first appearance on *The Steve Allen Show*—which was also my first appearance on television as a stand-up—I wore black pants and a bright blue marching-band coat I had picked up in a San Francisco thrift shop. Steve's introduction of me was ad-libbed perfectly. "This next young man is a comedian, and . . ." he stammered, ". . . at first you might not get it"—he stammered again—"but then you think about it for a while, and you still don't get it"—stammer, stammer—"then, you might want to come up onstage and talk to him about it."

The *Steve Allen* appearance went well—he loved the offbeat, and his cackle was enough to make any comedian feel confident. Seated on the sofa, though, I was hammered by another guest, *The Dick Van Dyke Show*'s Morey Amsterdam, for being unconventional. But I bore no grudge; I was so naive I didn't even know I had been insulted. The *Steve Allen* credit opened a few doors, and I bounced around all of the afternoon shows, juggling material, trying not to repeat myself. I developed a formula of convenience: "If I do a bit on *Merv Griffin*, which comes on at two P.M., it's okay to repeat the material on *Virginia Graham*, which comes on at four P.M. If I do a piece on *Steve Allen*, which comes on at five P.M. on Wednesdays, I can do the same bit on *Mike Douglas*, which comes on at three P.M. on Fridays." Or something like that. Through the three or four years I did these shows, I appeared probably fifty times.

I recently viewed a musty video of an appearance on *The Virginia Graham Show*, circa 1970, unseen since its airing. I looked grotesque. I had a hairdo like a helmet, which I blow-dried to a puffy bouffant, for reasons I no longer understand. I wore a frock coat and a silk shirt, and my delivery was mannered, slow, and self-aware. I had absolutely no authority. After reviewing the show, I was—especially since I was writing an autobiography documenting my success—depressed for a week. But later, searching my mind for at least one redeeming quality in the performance, I became aware that not one joke was normal, that even though I was the one who said the lines, I did not know what was coming next. The audience might have thought what I am thinking now: "Was that terrible? Or was it good?"

Weird hair on *The Virginia Graham Show.*

FROM THESE TELEVISION APPEARANCES, I got a welcome job in 1971 with Ann-Margret, five weeks opening the show for her at the International Hilton in Vegas, a huge, unfunny barn with sculptured pink cherubs hanging from the corners of the proscenium. Laughter in these poorly designed places rose a few feet into the air and dissipated like steam, always giving me the feeling I was bombing. One night, from my dressing room, I saw a vision in white gliding down the hall—a tall, striking woman, moving like an apparition along the backstage corridor. It turned out to be Priscilla Presley, coming to visit Ann-Margret backstage after having seen the show. When she turned the corner, she revealed an even more indelible presence walking behind her. Elvis. Dressed in white. Jet-black hair. A diamond-studded buckle.

When Priscilla revealed Elvis to me, I was also revealed to Elvis. I'm sure he noticed that this twenty-five-year-old stick figure was frozen firmly to the ground. About to pass me by, Elvis stopped, looked at me, and said in his beautiful Mississippi drawl: "Son, you have an ob-leek sense of humor."

Later, after his visit with Ann-Margret, he stopped by my dressing room and told Bill and me that he, too, had an oblique sense of humor—which he did—but that his audience didn't get it. Then he said, "Do you want to see my guns?" After emptying the bullets into his palm, he showed us two pistols and a derringer.

Ann-Margret and her husband, Roger Smith, were, and still are, a fun and generous couple, and they provided me with work when others wouldn't. The next year they asked if I would open for Ann-Margret at the Fontainebleau Hotel in Miami Beach. I arrived at the hotel, which at the time was very old-world, with an even older clientele. I still had my helmet hair, long black frock coat, and turquoise jewelry, and I'd added a really unattractive beard. Opening night, I peeked at the audience. Older Jewish couples. I smelled disaster. Jerry Lewis once described standing backstage before a show and, listening to the tone of the audience, concluding: "I knew I was dead." I could hear the echoing rattle of forks on plates and the low, enervated dinner chitchat. I went on . . . and killed. Night after night. I was going over like it was a raucous college campus. Why? I wondered. I was baffled until Roger Smith explained it to me. "They look at you in your hippie clothes and beard and think, 'Aw, it's my son.'"

THE PLUM TELEVISION APPEARANCE during the sixties and seventies was *The Tonight Show Starring Johnny Carson.* Bob Shayne, who in the late sixties booked *The Steve Allen Show,* had moved over to *The Tonight Show* and mentioned me to its producer, Freddy De Cordova. Bob showed Freddy a kinescope (an expensive sixteen-millimeter film financed by my bank account) of my appearance on *The Steve Allen Show,* and Fred replied, "I don't think he's for us." But Bob persisted, and Johnny saw the film and said, "Let's give him a try." To close the deal, I went to NBC one afternoon and auditioned on the soundstage, in front of staff and crew, while cables were being pulled and cameras were being moved. I was booked on the show in October 1972.

There was a belief that one appearance on *The Tonight Show* made you a star. But here are the facts. The first time you do the show, nothing. The second time you do the show, nothing. The sixth time you do the show, someone

125

might come up to you and say, "Hi, I think we met at Harry's Christmas party." The tenth time you do the show, you could conceivably be remembered as being seen somewhere on television. The twelfth time you do the show, you might hear, "Oh, I know you. You're that guy."

But I didn't know that. Before the show, as I stood in the backstage darkness behind the curtain of *The Tonight Show*, hearing the muffled laughter while Johnny spoke and waiting for the tap on the shoulder that would tell me I was on, an italicized sentence ticker-taped through my head: "*I am about to do* The Tonight Show." Then I walked out onstage, started my act, and thought, "*I am doing* The Tonight Show." I finished my act and thought, "*I have just done* The Tonight Show." What happened while I was out there was very similar to an alien abduction: I remember very little of it, though I'm convinced it occurred.

I was booked back and did the show successfully several times. I was doing material from my act, best stuff first, and after two or three appearances, I realized how little best stuff I had. After I'd gone through my stage material, I started doing some nice but oddball bits such as Comedy Act for Dogs (first done on *Steve Allen*), in which I said, "A lot of dogs watch TV but there's really nothing on for them, so call your dog over and let him watch because I think you're going to see him crack up for the first time." Then I brought out four dogs "that I can perform to so I can get the timing down." While I did terrible canine-related jokes, the dogs would walk off one at a time, with the last dog lifting his leg on me. The studio audience saw several trainers out of camera range, making drastic hand signals, but the home TV audience saw only the dogs doing their canine best.

Another time I claimed that I could read from the phone book and make it funny. I opened the book and droned the names to the predictable silence, then I pretended to grow more and more desperate and began to do retro shtick such as cracking eggs on my head. I got word that Johnny was not thrilled, and I was demoted to appearing with guest hosts, which I tried not to admit to myself was a devastating blow.

I WAS GROWING FRUSTRATED with writing for television. Although the income was financing my performing career, I was marking time, and the prize of performing regularly on one of the shows was not materializing. I realized that the performers were just using my material as a starting point and, of course, I thought the better joke was to do it as written. On *The Sonny & Cher Comedy Hour*, I was thrown the occasional performing bone, appearing as a walk-on with a line or two in a sketch, but I felt no resonance from the producers or audience. There was a baffling moment when Sonny Bono and his partner, Denis Pregnolato, who were becoming showbiz entrepreneurs, approached me at work and took me aside. Sonny and Denis had seen me perform—I don't know where—and

Sonny said, "Steve, we've been watching you. We think you are the next big thing, bigger than David Brenner, bigger than Albert Brooks. We would like to work with you and develop a show for you." I nodded my excitement and never heard from them again, not one word.

In the early seventies, I had two memorable auditions. One was for Greg Garrison, the producer of *The Dean Martin Show*. The audition went like this: I did my act for his secretary, then she did it for Greg. She even borrowed a prop from me to take into his office. My other audition began with a call from a producer who told me about a sitcom pilot called *The Fireman's Ball*. "They specifically asked for you," he said. I heard this sentence as "They specifically asked *only* for you." I practiced the scene, went to the audition, and was surprised to see at least a dozen other young guys marching around a foyer holding scripts and inaudibly mouthing their lines. I didn't get hired, but the experience was significant for me. I understood I would never be hired in that situation, that the odds of confluence on a certain day of the producers' desires, my talent, and a good reading were low, and that the audition process was a dead end. I decided to leave Hollywood and go on the road.

I resigned from television writing against the advice of my agent, a man who had wisely vacuumed up all the young talent discovered by the Smothers Brothers. He said plainly, "Stick to writing." Which was a polite way of saying that my performing was headed nowhere. I took this warning with a strange delight. It was, in a way, the necessary ingredient in any young career, like when Al Jolson was told in *The Jazz Singer*, "Jolie, you'll never become a sing-gah!"

Bill McEuen had moved to Aspen, Colorado, for the skiing, and I moved to Santa Fe, New Mexico, to escape the Los Angeles smog and traffic. I was twenty-eight years old when a bleak thought occurred to me: "What if nothing happens?" I had never really imagined success; I was just trying to be a performer, but I could not see myself playing dreary nightclubs into my thirties, forties, and fifties. I would have struggled composing a real-world résumé, as my abilities were at best vague and at worst unusable. I decided to give it until I was thirty, and then I would have to figure out something else to do.

The Road

MY DEPARTURE FROM TELEVISION WRITING meant that I was now adrift. I had lost my financial support and my hyphen and now was only a comedian. A club owner in Denver, Chet Hansen, started up a small agency, and even though comedy clubs did not exist yet, he somehow produced wide-ranging bookings that involved planes, trains, and automobiles. For the next few years, I was on the road with an itinerary designed by the Marquis de Sade. But there was a sexy anonymity about the travel; I was living the folkie myth of having no ties to anyone, working small clubs and colleges in improvised folk rooms that were usually subterranean. However, the travel isolated me. Friends were available only through costly phone calls, and contact with my parents and sister spiraled down to a pinpoint.

In this netherworld, I was free to experiment. These out-of-the-way and varied places provided a tough comedy education. There were no mentors to tell me what to do; there were no guidebooks for doing stand-up. Everything was learned in practice, and the lonely road, with no critical eyes watching, was the place to dig up my boldest, or dumbest, ideas and put them onstage. At night, preoccupied by the success or failure of that evening's show, I would return to my motel room and glumly watch the three TV channels sign off the air at eleven-thirty, knowing I had at least two more hours of ceiling staring to do before the adrenaline eased off and I could fall asleep.

While I toured around the country, Bill had found a Los Angeles agent whom we both adored: Marty Klein. Marty, who loved gold cigarette lighters, fancy eyeglasses, and quality suits, made sure I saw the old-time world of show business before it was gone, taking me to the Brown Derby restaurant in Hollywood, where the walls were lined with celebrity caricatures from the thirties and forties, and the Sands Hotel in Vegas, where the Rat Pack had cavorted. Bill was also promoting my name to record companies. A recording contract was our quest, though I secretly worried about a record's potential, as my act was becoming more and more visual. "And now," I would announce, "my impression of the Incredible Shrinking Man!" I would ask the audience to close their eyes for a

132
—

moment, and when they reopened them, I had raised the microphone several feet. Another bit: I would wonder what it would be like if the human body had only one arm right in the center of our chest. How would we applaud? Putting my elbow in the center of my torso, I would then slap myself in the face a dozen times.

I took on an excellent roadie, Maple Byrne, whom I met at a defunct recording studio where he lived in the echo chamber. He was a real Deadhead who had to vanish now and then to see a Grateful Dead concert. He booked my travel, set up the props, checked the sound, and ran the lights. Despite his presence, on the road I was fundamentally a loner, withdrawn and solitary, and his introduction of mournful Irish folk music into my life didn't help my mood. We would drive at night from job to job, listening to cassette tapes of the Bothy Band. Sad, lonely songs for the sad, lonely road. One of the tunes, "The Maid of Coolmore," inspired a film I wrote twelve years later, *L.A. Story*.

When necessary, I could still manage to have a personality, and sometimes I was rescued by a local girl who actually liked me. Occasionally the result was an erotic tryst enhanced by loneliness. Perhaps the women saw it as I did, an encounter free from obligation: the next day I would be gone. I had also refined my pickup technique. If I knew I would be returning to a club, I tweaked my hard-learned rule, "Never hit on a waitress the first night," to "Never hit on a waitress for six months." I came

133

off as coolly reserved, as I would harmlessly flirt on my first visit; by my next visit, everything was in place. Soon the six months caught up with me, and I always had someone I could latch on to as I rolled from town to town.

I did have interludes of monogamy with a few women. Iris C. was an aspiring actress who, coincidentally, lived next door, which cut down on travel time for sudden sleepover urges. Chris Gooch, a fragile, ethereal blonde, seemed to float into the club I was playing, the Vanguard, in Kansas City, Missouri. We lived together in Los Angeles for a while. Sandee Oliver—her last name described the color of her skin—lived in Atlanta, and we rendezvoused in towns across America. Were they beautiful? We were all beautiful. We were in our twenties.

I alternated obscure appearances across America with higher-profile opening-act jobs at the Boarding House in San Francisco, the Troubadour in Los Angeles, and the Great Southeast Music Hall in Atlanta, where I first performed with the singer/comedian Martin Mull. Martin's wit was Sahara-dry; he performed onstage sitting on living room furniture and sang his own comic songs, with titles like "Noses Run in My Family," "I'm Everyone I Ever Loved," "(How Could I Not Miss) A Girl Your Size," and "Jesus Christ, Football Star." On opening night at the Great Southeast Music Hall, we were both nervous about meeting each other. I was sitting in my open dressing room when Martin walked by, carrying his stage clothes on a hanger. Unsure whether to say something to me, he

134
—

kept going. After a few steps, I called out, "Nice meeting you, too." We've been friends ever since.

Martin suggested me to his recording label, Capricorn Records. The response from the producer, Phil Walden, was "Too visual; he's too visual." Later, after my first record shipped platinum (meaning it had already sold a million before it was released), Phil called up Martin: "Hey, Mull, you know any more of those visual guys?"

Yes, I suppose I was visual.

In Los Angeles, the Troubadour was my hangout, and the girls did indeed get prettier as closing time neared, or maybe it was I who got prettier to them. The Troubadour's regulars included Michael Nesmith, Jackson Browne, Joni Mitchell, Glenn Frey, Don Henley, and all the others whose music was a siren call to a perceptive record executive named David Geffen. One week I opened the show for Linda Ronstadt; she sang barefoot on a raised stage and wore a silver lamé dress that stopped a millimeter below her panties, causing the floor of the Troubadour to be slick with drool. Linda and I saw each other for a while, but I was so intimidated by her talent and street smarts that, after the ninth date, she finally said, "Steve, do you often date girls and not try to sleep with them?" We parted chaste.

One late night I was lingering in the bar and talking to Glenn Frey, who was just leaving his duo, Longbranch Pennywhistle. He said he was considering a name for his new five-man group. "What is it?" I said. He said, "Eagles." I said, "You mean, *the* Eagles." He said, "No, Eagles." I said, "You mean, *the* Eagles?" He said, "No, I mean Eagles." The name of the group remains, of course, Eagles.

Mixed reviews continued. At the end of my closing-night show at the Troubadour, I stood onstage and took out five bananas. I peeled them, put one on my head, one in each pocket, and squeezed one in each hand. Then I read the last line of my latest bad review: "Sharing the bill with Poco this week is comedian Steve

Linda onstage at the Troubadour.

Martin . . . his twenty-five-minute routine failed to establish any comic identity that would make the audience remember him or the material." Then I walked off the stage.

IN CASE I AD-LIBBED something wonderful, I began taping my shows with a chintzy cassette recorder. I had a

The Troubadour, 1968.

routine in which I played a smug party guy with a drink in his hand. When the bit started, the waitresses brought me a glass of wine that I would use as a prop. When that glass was empty, they would bring me another. One night I listened to the tape and could hear myself slurring. I never had a drink before or during a show again.

I made another correction based on the tapes. Texas-born and California-raised, I realized I was dropping my "ings"—runnin', walkin', and talkin'—and I worked like Eliza Doolittle to elevate my speech. It was a struggle; at first I thought I sounded pretentious and unnatural. But I did it, though now and then I slip back into my natural way of speakin'.

THE CONSISTENT WORK enhanced my act. I learned a lesson: It was easy to be great. Every entertainer has a night when everything is clicking. These nights are accidental and statistical: Like lucky cards in poker, you can count on them occurring over time. What was hard was to be *good*, consistently good, night after night, no matter what the abominable circumstances. Performing in so many varied situations made every predicament manageable, from Toronto, where I performed next to an active salad bar, to the well-paying but soul-killing Playboy Clubs, where I was almost but not quite able to go over. But as I continued to work, my material grew; I came up with odd little gags such as "How many people have never raised their hands before?" I was now capable of doing two different twenty-five-minute sets per evening, in case some of the audience stayed over for the second show.

Because I was generally unknown, in the smaller venues I was free to gamble with material, and there were a few evenings when crucial mutations affected my developing act. At Vanderbilt University in Nashville, I played for approximately a hundred students in a classroom with a stage at one end. I did the show, and it went fine. However, when it was over, something odd happened. The audience didn't leave. The stage had no

139

wings, no place for me to go, but I still had to pack up my props. I indicated that the show had ended, but they just sat there, even after I said flatly, "It's over." They thought this was all part of the act, and I couldn't convince them otherwise. Then I realized there were no exits from the stage and that the only way out was to go through the audience. So I kept talking. I passed among them, ad-libbing comments along the way. I walked out into the hallway, trying to finish the show, but they followed me there, too. A reluctant pied piper, I went outside onto the campus, and they stayed right behind me. I came across a drained swimming pool. I asked the audience to get into it—"Everybody into the pool!"—and they did. Then I said I was going to swim across the top of them, and the crowd knew exactly what to do: I was passed hand over hand as I did the crawl. That night I went to bed feeling I had entered new comic territory. My show was becoming something else, something free and unpredictable, and the doing of it thrilled me, because each new performance brought my view of comedy into sharper focus.

The act tightened. It became more physical. It was true I couldn't sing or dance, but singing *funny* and dancing *funny* were another matter. All I had to do was free my mind and start. I would abruptly stop the show and sing loudly, in my best lounge-singer voice, "Grampa bought a rubber." Walking up to the mike, I would say, "Here's something you don't often see," and I'd spread my mouth

140

wide with my fingers and leap into the air while screaming. Or, invoking a remembered phrase from the magic
shop, I would shout, "Uh-oh, I'm getting happy feet!" and
then dance uncontrollably across the stage, my feet
moving like Balla's painting of a futurist dog, while my
face told the audience that I wanted to stop but couldn't.
Closing the show, I'd say, "I'd like to thank each and every
one of you for coming here tonight." Then I would walk
into the audience and, in fast motion, thank everyone in-
dividually. My set lists, written on notepad paper and kept
in my coat pocket, were becoming drenched with sweat.

The new physicality brought an unexpected element
into the act: precision. My routines wove the verbal with
the physical and I found pleasure trying to bring them in
line. Each spoken idea had to be physically expressed as
well. My teenage attempt at a magician's grace was being
transformed into an awkward comic grace. I felt as though
every part of me was working. Some nights it seemed that
it wasn't the line that got the laugh, but the tip of my finger.
I tried to make voice and posture as crucial as jokes and
gags. Silence, too, brought forth laughs. Sometimes I
would stop and, saying nothing, stare at the audience with
a look of mock disdain, and on a good night, it struck us all
as funny, as if we were in on the joke even though there
was no actual joke we could point to. Finally, I understood
the cummings quote I had puzzled over in college: "Like
the burlesque comedian, I am abnormally fond of that precision which creates movement." Precision was moving

the plot forward, was filling every moment with content, was keeping the audience engaged.

The act was becoming simultaneously smart and stupid. My version of smart was to imbue a hint of conceptualism into the whole affair: My sing-along had some funny lyrics, but it was also impossible to sing along with. My version of stupid: "Oh, gosh! My shoelace is untied!" I would bend down, see that my shoelace was not untied, stand up, and say, "Oh, I love playing jokes on myself!"

I had the plumber joke, which was impossible to understand even for plumbers:

"Okay, I don't like to gear my material to the audience, but I'd like to make an exception, because I was told that there is a convention of plumbers in town this week—I understand about thirty of them came down to the show tonight—so before I came out, I worked up a joke especially for the plumbers. Those of you who aren't plumbers probably won't get this and won't think it's funny, but I think those of you who are plumbers will really enjoy this.

"This lawn supervisor was out on a sprinkler maintenance job, and he started working on a Findlay sprinkler head with a Langstrom seven-inch gangly wrench. Just then this little apprentice leaned over and said, 'You can't work on a Findlay sprinkler head with a Langstrom seven-inch wrench.' Well, this infuriated the supervisor, so he went and got volume fourteen of the Kinsley manual, and he reads to him and says, 'The Langstrom seven-inch wrench can be used with the Findlay sprocket.' Just then the little apprentice leaned over and says, 'It says sprocket, not socket!'

[*Worried pause.*]

"Were these plumbers supposed to be here this show?"

One of my favorite bits to perform evolved at the Troubadour in Los Angeles. After I finished my act, I would go up to the sound booth, where there was an open mike out of sight of the audience, and say, "They can't hear me out there, can they?" "No," the coached soundman would reply. Then I would say, "What a bunch of assholes. Where can I get some pot?" I would continue my arrogant comments until the bit ran dry.

On the road, the daylight hours moved slowly, filled with aimless wandering through malls and museums. But at night, onstage, *every second mattered. Every gesture mattered.* The few hours I spent in the clubs and coffeehouses seemed like a full existence.

When I had new material to try, I would break it down into its smallest elements, literally a gesture or a few words, then sneak it into the act in its shortest form, being careful not to disrupt the flow of the show. If it worked, the next night I would add the next discreet packet until the bit either filled out or died. I can remember bailing out of a bit because I didn't want to be trapped in it for the next five minutes. The easiest way was to pre-

143

tend I'd gotten distracted by something and then completely change tack.

Around this time I smelled a rat. The rat was the Age of Aquarius. Though the era's hairstyles, clothes, and lingo still dominated youth culture, by 1972 the movement was tired and breaking down. Drugs had killed people, and so had Charles Manson. The war in Vietnam was near its official end, but its devastating losses had embittered and divided America. The political scene was exhausting, and many people, including me, were alienated from government. Murders and beatings at campus protests weren't going to be resolved by sticking a daisy into the pointy end of a rifle. Flower Power was waning, but no one wanted to believe it yet, because we had all invested so much of ourselves in its message. Change was imminent.

I cut my hair, shaved my beard, and put on a suit. I stripped the act of all political references, which I felt was an act of defiance. To politics I was saying, "I'll get along without you very well. It's time to be funny." Overnight, I was no longer at the tail end of an old movement but at the front end of a new one. Instead of looking like another freak with a crazy act, I now looked like a visitor from the straight world who had gone seriously awry. The act's unbridled nonsense was taking the audience—and me—on a wild ride, and my growing professionalism, founded on thousands of shows, created a subliminal sense of authority that made the audience feel they weren't being had.

144
—

Between 1973 and 1975, my one-man vaudeville show turned fully toward the surreal. I was linking the unlink-able, blending economy and extravagance, non sequiturs with the conventional. I was all over the place, sluicing the gold from the dirt, honing the edge that confidence

Cut my hair, put on a suit.

brings. I cannot say I was fearless, because I was acutely aware of any audience drift, and if I sensed trouble, I would swerve around it. I believed it was important to be funny now, while the audience was watching, but it was also important to be funny later, when the audience was home and thinking about it. I didn't worry if a bit got no response, as long as I believed it had enough strangeness to linger. My friend Rick Moranis (whose imitation of Woody Allen was so precise that it made

145

Woody seem like a faker) called my act's final manifestation "anti-comedy."

ONE WEEKEND I WAS PLAYING at the Boarding House in San Francisco, opening for a talented mountain-man folksinger named U. Utah Philips. My shows went well, very well. I waited for the reviews, but there was scant mention. Five paragraphs devoted to Utah, and a line or two about me. I noticed it in Los Angeles, too, at the Troubadour. Large thoughtful reviews of the headliner, little or nothing about the opening act. I was learning something about the audience and critics: They aren't there to see the opener. The implied power of the headliner cannot be challenged by a pleasant opening act. But I was not a headliner; I had no following, and I was nearing my arbitrary thirty-year cutoff point. I was consistently appearing on TV shows, even *The Tonight Show,* but what filled folk clubs was underground word of mouth, usually generated by record sales, not late-night TV watchers. I decided to headline only, win or lose. This meant no more Boarding House, no more Troubadour. It meant that the size of the house I could play would drop significantly. I held firmly to this idea, and within the year, I was completely broke.

I called the comedian David Brenner for advice. David was successfully guest-hosting *The Tonight Show* and filling theaters and clubs. Our paths had crossed, and we had exchanged phone numbers. I explained that I was getting jobs, but the travel costs were killing me. If I got five hundred dollars for an appearance, it would cost me three hundred just to get to it. He told me the deal he always proposed to club owners. He would take the door, and they would take the bar. He said he would hire someone to stand at the entrance with a mechanical counter to make sure he wasn't being cheated. I didn't have the chutzpah to "audit" this way, but otherwise it seemed like a fair gambit. I wanted to either get in or get out of the business. I would be paid according to how many people I drew, and that satisfied my Protestant inclination to earn my keep.

I proposed this deal immediately to an amenable club owner—after all, he didn't have to put any money up front—and in October 1973 I got a job at Bubbas in Coconut Grove, Florida, now vanished into the folkie sinkhole. It held about ninety people, seated in the worst configuration a club could have. Directly in front of the stage were seats for about ten; extending to the performer's right were the other eighty seats. There was no depth at all, and most of the audience saw only a side view of the performer. These lopsided arrangements were never conducive to laughter because the audience couldn't quite unite. I arrived a day early, in time to see the closing night of another performer, a comedian who, at least in the show I saw, lifted a line or two from Lenny Bruce. Doing other people's material was on my taboo list, but he was a nice

147

guy and still funny, and when we met after the show, he knew that I knew that he knew that I knew, but we ignored it.

The next night I opened, and business was slow. However, I was ready to put my experience at Vanderbilt into effect. The Florida night was balmy and I was able to take the audience outside into the street and roam around in front of the club, making wisecracks. I didn't quite know how to end the show. First I started hitchhiking; a few cars passed me by. Then a taxi came by. I hailed it and got in. I went around the block, returned and waved at the audience—still standing there—then drove off and never came back. The next morning I received one of the most crucial reviews of my life. John Huddy, the respected entertainment critic for *The Miami Herald,* devoted his entire column to my act. Without qualification, he raved in paragraph after paragraph, starting with HE PARADES HIS HILARITY RIGHT OUT INTO THE STREET, and concluded with: "Steve Martin is the brightest, cleverest, wackiest new comedian around." Oh, and the next night the club owner made sure all tabs had been paid before I took the audience outside.

Roger Smith had told me that when he came to Hollywood from El Paso to be an actor, he had given himself six months to get work. The time elapsed, and he packed up his car, which was parked on Sunset Boulevard, where his final audition would be. Informed that he was not right for the job, he went out and started up his car. He was about to

BUBBAS

2990 Grand Avenue
Coconut Grove

FINE·FOOD BEER WINE

for reservations
call 444-9582

live music
mon. thru sat.!

Playbill~ oct. 1-13

Steve Goodman
oct. 1~6 (mon.~sat.)

City of New Orleans has been called "the best damned train song ever written"~ and Steve Goodman wrote it. He's one of the current "Chicago Gang" of singers/writers, and his music is that special blend of down-home country fun and sophisticated blues called urban folk. Steve records for Buddah Records (Kristofferson produced his first album). Come in and hear him~ he's something special.

Steve Martin
oct. 8-13 (mon.~sat.)

credits: Midnight Special
In Concert
Tonight (Johnny Carson)
Merv Griffin Show
Mike Douglas Show
The Bitter End (New York)
The Ice House (Passadena)
~ he's also written for~
Sonny and Cher
The Smothers Brothers
Glen Campbell

~ just your ordinary banjo magic act.

Vince Martin
oct. 1~2 (mon.~tues.)

a Coconut Grove legend ~
back again, better than ever!

Teri De Sario
oct. 8~9 (mon.~tues.)

young and fresh and beautiful and very talented ~
you'll fall in love with Teri ~ and her music!

Mike & Barbara Smith~
oct. 3-6, 10-13
(wed.~sat. both weeks)

if you've caught the shows at Bubba's recently, you probably know and love Mike and Barbara already~ if not, you're in for a real treat! You won't find better entertainment anywhere ~as good~maybe but not better!

~ shows: mon.~fri. 8:30 & 11:00, sat. 9:30 & 12:00 ~

The flyer at Bubbas. Steve Goodman played the week before me, and later he became a sensational opening act for my show.

BORN STANDING UP

pull away, away to El Paso, when there was a knock on his windshield. "We saw you in the hall. Would you like to read for us?" the voice said. He was then cast as the star of the hit television show 77 *Sunset Strip*. My review from John Huddy was the knock on the window just as I was about to get in my car and drive to a metaphorical El Paso, and it gave me a psychological boost that allowed me to nix my arbitrarily chosen thirty-year-old deadline to reenter the conventional world. The next night and the rest of the week the club was full, all ninety seats. Three thousand miles away, Bill McEuen took the review and waved it in the face of every record executive in Hollywood, with no bites.

I continued to appear on *The Tonight Show*, always with a guest host, doing material I was developing on the road. Then I got a surprise note from Bob Shayne: "We had a meeting with Johnny yesterday, told him you'd been a smash twice with guest hosts, and he agrees you should be back on with him. So I think that hurdle is over." In September 1974 I was booked on the show with Johnny.

This was welcome news. Johnny had comic savvy. The daytime television hosts, with the exception of Steve Allen, did not come from comedy. I had a small routine (suggested by my writer friend Michael Elias) that went like this: "I just bought a new car. It's a prestige car. A '65 Greyhound bus. You know you can get up to thirty tons of luggage in one of those babies? I put a lot of money into it. . . . I put a new dog on the side. And if I said to a girl,

150

'Do you want to get in the backseat?' I had, like, forty chances." Etc. Not great, but at the time it was working. It did, however, require all the pauses and nuance that I could muster. On *The Merv Griffin Show* I decided to use it for panel, meaning I would sit with Merv and pretend it was just chat. I began: "I just bought a new car. A '65 Greyhound bus." Merv, friendly as ever, interrupted and said, "Now, why on earth would you buy a Greyhound bus?" I had no prepared answer; I just stared at him. I thought, "Oh my God, because it's a comedy routine." And the bit was dead. Johnny, on the other hand, was the comedian's friend. He waited; he gave you your timing. He lay back and stepped in like Ali, not to knock you out but to set you up. He struggled with you, too, and sometimes saved you.

I was able to maintain a personal relationship with Johnny over the next thirty years, at least as personal as he or I could make it, and I was flattered that he came to respect my comedy. On one of my appearances, after he had done a solid impression of Goofy the cartoon dog, he leaned over to me during a commercial and whispered prophetically, "You'll use everything you ever knew." He was right; twenty years later I did my teenage rope tricks in the movie *¡Three Amigos!*

Once Johnny joked in his monologue, "I announced that I was going to write my autobiography, and nineteen publishers went out and copyrighted the title *Cold and Aloof.*" This was the common perception of him. But

151

Johnny was not aloof; he was polite. He did not presume intimate relationships where there were none; he took time, and with time grew trust. He preserved his dignity by maintaining the personality that was appropriate for him.

Johnny enjoyed the delights of split-second timing, of watching a comedian squirm and then rescue himself, of the surprises that can arise in the seconds of desperation when the comedian senses that his joke might fall to silence. Johnny was inclined toward the sciences, especially astronomy, and his Nebraskan pragmatism—and knowledge of magicians' tricks—guaranteed that the occultists, future predictors, spoon benders, and mind readers never left his show without a challenge. He knew the difference between the pompous ass and the nervous actress and who should receive appropriate consideration. He enjoyed the unflappable grannies who sewed log-cabin quilts, as well as the Vegas pro who machine-gunned the audience into hysterical fits. Johnny hosted authors, children, intellects, and nitwits and treated them all well, and he served the audience with his curiosity and tolerance. He gave each guest—like the ideal America would—the benefit of the doubt: You're nuts, but you're welcome here.

For my first show back, I chose to do a bit I had developed years earlier at the Ice House. I speed-talked a Vegas nightclub act in two minutes. Appearing on the show was Sammy Davis, Jr., who, while still performing energetically, had also become a historic showbiz figure. I was whizzing along, singing a four-second version of "Ebb Tide," then saying at lightning speed, "Frank Sinatra personal friend of mine Sammy Davis Jr. personal friend of mine Steve Martin I'm a personal friend of mine too and now a little dancin'!" I started a wild flail, which I must say was pretty funny, when a showbiz miracle occurred. The camera cut away to a dimly lit Johnny, precisely as he whirled up from his chair, doubling over with laughter. Suddenly, subliminally, I was endorsed. At the end of the act, Sammy came over and hugged me. I felt like I hadn't been hugged since I was born.

This was my sixteenth appearance on the show, and

On *The Tonight Show* with Johnny and Sammy.

153

the first one I could really call a smash. The next day, elated by my success, I walked into an antique store on La Brea. The woman behind the counter looked at me.

"Are you that boy who was on *The Tonight Show* last night?"

"Yes," I said.

"Yuck!" she blurted out.

Breakthrough

I DID HAVE A TINY BIT of drawing power, generated through my daytime television appearances and my growing presence on *The Tonight Show,* but mostly my name was a rumor. My dubious status as a headliner led me to a tiny pie slice of a folk club in Greenwich Village, the Metro. Now *I* had an opening act. Still, no one showed up to see me and a new duo, Lindsey Buckingham and Stevie Nicks. I told the club owner that he could let me go if he wanted, that I wouldn't hold him to his contract. He said he wanted me to stay . . . until the next night, when again no one showed up. We parted with a handshake.

In March 1975 my agent, Marty Klein, secured a job in San Francisco, two weeks headlining the Playboy Club for fifteen hundred dollars per week. A big payday, and I was desperate for money. Playboy Clubs always made me nervous. I never seemed to do well in them, but I had no choice. Opening night was on a Monday, which was already unusual; clubs were usually closed on Mondays. I stood at the back of the club and checked out the capacity crowd. Amazed, I said to one of the musicians leaning against the wall, "We got a nice house out there." An odd look crossed the musician's face. "Yeah," he said mysteriously.

156

After I was introduced as Steve Miller, I walked out

onstage and saw a sea of Japanese faces. I attempted a few lines; nothing came back except nice smiles. No one spoke English. It turned out that the bus tours offered a night-club as part of their packages, but on Mondays the Play-boy Club was the only one open, so every foreign tour group was herded into this showroom. Now I understood the musician's wry grin. I gamely went forward, not doing badly because the audience was kind and polite, and my balloon-animal and magic act went over well because it was visual and antic. The next night I went on for the reg-ular audience: death. Comedy Death. Which is worse than regular death. I sank low and, in spite of my declining financial situation, called Marty, saying, "You've got to get me out of here." He did, and I went back the next night to collect my things. My clothes had been stolen. A week later, I took out a bank loan of five thousand dollars.

The euphoria from my week at Bubbas in Coconut Grove and my nice score on *The Tonight Show* had dissi-pated, and I was marooned in the depression that fol-lowed my flop at the Playboy Club. In June 1975 I was booked into the frighteningly named Hub Pub Club, in Winston-Salem, North Carolina. The Hub Pub Club, lo-cated in a shopping mall, was trying to be a fancy spot for gentlemen, but the liquor laws in North Carolina limited attendance at nightclubs to members only. About the worst things an entertainer can hear are "members only" and "group tours." While I was onstage doing my act to churchlike silence, a guy said to his date, loud enough that we all heard it, "I don't understand any of this." And at that moment, neither did I.

In spite of the gloom, I had a premonition of success, and in January 1975 I started a short-lived diary. It surprises me that a diary meant to chronicle an important year in my life could contain so many negative passages. My entry for the Hub Pub Club started this way: "This town smells like a cigarette." Then I sank a bit lower: "My material seems so old. The audience indulged me during the second show." Then I really started wallowing in it: "My act might have well been in a foreign language . . . my act has no ending." Next I degenerated into my version of Kurtz's lament, "The horror, the horror," from *Heart of Darkness*: "My new material is hopelessly poor. My act is simply not good enough—it's not even bad."

However, there was one, sole, positive entry in my journal that week. It related to a lonely-guy phone call I had made to a new acquaintance, Victoria Dailey. Victoria was a young rare-book-and-print dealer in Los Angeles whom I had stumbled upon in my collecting quests, and who had her wits about her in the same way that Oscar Wilde had his wits about him. I must have had an intuition about the future depth and scope of our relationship, as I called her long distance from a motel phone, which in those days cost about a million dollars a minute. While traffic whizzed by outside the gray motel room, I churned out my Winston-Salem stories with the same toxicity as the R. J. Reynolds company churned out cigarettes. Victoria used her refined sense of artistic ethics to talk me down from my metaphorical window ledge, and over the next few years we cemented an enduring relationship that has been complex and rewarding. We have been connected over the past thirty years intellectually, aesthetically, and seemingly, gravitationally. In my latest conversation with her, I complimented her recent essay on early Southern California history. I said, "Do you realize you're going to be studied one day?" She replied, "Only one day?"

Two months after Winston-Salem everything was about to change. A few blocks away from San Francisco's Playboy Club, where I had died so swiftly, was a very different kind of club, one that booked current music acts, and where the waitresses were sexy but didn't have to wear bunny outfits. I had played the Boarding House before, but only as a developing opening act. The owner, David Allen, saw that things were different, both with my act and with its reception, and he was ready to try the new and improved me. In August 1975 I was booked to headline, evidence that the Boarding House and the Playboy Club did not speak to each other. My years on the road had produced a change I had only dreamed of earlier: I now had four hours of material from which to pick and choose, and there was more to come.

I opened at the Boarding House on a Tuesday evening to a fair-sized crowd. Headlining there, in friendly and familiar San Francisco, where I had established some kind of beachhead, filled me and the audience with confidence. They had paid to see this show, this particular show, and I was inspired to push the limits even further. What had been deadly at the Playboy Clubs was lively with a younger crowd. I wanted the audience to leave with the feeling that something had happened. The first few minutes into the show, I began to strum the banjo, singing a song that had no particular tune or rhyme:

We're having some fun
We've got music and laughter
And wonderful times

That's so important in today's world

Oh yeah.

It's so hard to laugh
It seems that short of tripping a nun
Nothing is funny anymore

But you know
I see people going to college
For fourteen years
Studying to be doctors and lawyers
And I see people going to work
At the drugstore at 7:30 every morning

To sell Flair pens

Onstage at the Boarding House.

But the most amazing thing to me is
I get paid
For doing
This.

Midweek, before the show, I told the spotlight operator not to change the light no matter how urgently I asked him to do it. Then, onstage, I made a small request for some mood lighting, a blue spotlight. The light stayed white. I slowly grew more and more angry. "Please," I said, "I would really like a blue spot. It's for the mood-lighting thing." I got very serious and murmured under my breath, "I can't even get a light change." John McEuen was sitting in the light booth that night. He said the operator began to believe me and moved to change the spot, but John stopped him. Soon it became clear that it was a gag, because I was reaching new levels of anger as I said how disgusting it was "that I, this entertainer who keeps *giving, and giving and giving, and keeps on giving,* can't seem to get a simple blue spotlight!" The bit ended at an exaggerated level of madness, with me screaming another phrase from my past, *"Well, excuuuse me,"* turning four syllables into about twenty. The audience response was nice enough, but I was surprised weeks later when I heard this expression coming back to me on the streets. It surprised me even more when in another few years it became a ubiquitous catchphrase.

Toward the end of the Boarding House show, I stepped off the stage, saying: "I just want to come down into the audience with my people . . . DON'T TOUCH ME!" I took them into the lobby, where there was an old-fashioned grand staircase. One of the doormen, a very likable and funny guy named Larry who had seen my show all week, happened to come in from the street, carrying a pair of pants on a hanger fresh from the dry cleaner. I looked at him, and he looked back, knowing he was in for it. He had a great sense of humor and didn't mind a bit. I said disdainfully, "Oh, it's Cleanpants. Mr. Cleanpants. You think your pants are so CLEAN. Well, CLEANPANTS, we don't need your type around here. . . . WAIT, CLEANPANTS . . . where ya going? You think you don't need us because your PANTS ARE SO CLEAN?" A better comic foil could not have been found; I still can see Larry standing there holding his dry cleaning and accepting the fake lambasting with bemused patience. And the audience, crowded together in the stairwell and mezzanine, ate it up.

MY SISTER, MELINDA, had gotten married and was raising her two children in San Jose, an hour's drive from San Francisco. My communication with her over the past decade had been minimal. She had made efforts to connect, but my travel kept sweeping me away, and I was most comfortable in the world I had made, detached from home ties. When I first became an uncle, I could have used a self-help book, *So Now You're an Uncle*. Melinda showed up at one of these Boarding House performances, and we visited after the show. It turned out she had been proudly monitoring my career from a distance, saving reviews and magazine stories, but our relationship, because of my familial ineptness, remained awkward and was not yet ready to bloom.

Bill McEuen dragged his Nagra up to San Francisco and started taping my shows in hopes of crafting a record from the material. John Wasserman, the critic at the *San Francisco Chronicle*, offered a rave of the Boarding House appearance that was so enticing it made *me* want to see the show. At the end of the week, I was handed my percentage of the gate, an envelope containing forty-five hundred dollars in cash, a sum I had never seen in one place before, much less in my needy and greedy palm. I walked home in the dark toward my room at the Hotel Commodore—still lugging my banjo, which I never let out of my sight—and fortunately, I was not mugged. There was something about that walk in the night that recalled my contemplative mood of nine years earlier, when I sat in darkness, just a few miles away at the Coffee Gallery, with absolutely no prospects. But now I was about to enter a phase of my life when three things would occur: I would earn money; I would grow to be famous; and I would be the funniest I ever was.

AFTER THE BOARDING HOUSE GIG, I was booked into a club in Nashville called the Exit/In. It was a low-ceilinged box, painted black inside, with two noisy smoke eaters hanging from the ceiling, to no avail. The dense secondhand smoke was being inhaled and exhaled, making it thirdhand and fourthhand smoke. The stage was perfectly situated in the corner of the room.

When I was performing, I could touch the ceiling with my hand, and I had to be careful when jumping onstage not to knock myself out. I was selling tickets without the usual requirement of hit records. The audience was there by word of mouth only, so everything they saw me do was new. The room seated about two hundred and fifty, and the shows were oversold, riotous and packed tight, which verified a growing belief of mine about comedy: The more physically uncomfortable the audience, the bigger the laughs. I continued closing the show by performing outside, which had an auxiliary effect of emptying out the house so the second show could begin. One night at the Exit/In I took the crowd down the street to a McDonald's and ordered three hundred hamburgers to go, then quickly changed it to one bag of fries. Another night, I took them to a club across the street and we watched another act. I was a new-enough performer that there was no overblown celebrity worship, which meant I could do the show and carouse in the streets, uninterrupted by ill-timed requests for autographs or photos. Even though I had done the act hundreds of times, it became new to me this hot, muggy week in Nashville. The disparate elements I'd begun with ten years before had become unified; my road experience had made me tough as steel, and I had total command of my material. But most important, I felt really, really funny.

165

I MOVED TO ASPEN, COLORADO, to be closer to my pals Bill McEuen and the Dirt Band. It was there, on the night of October 11, 1975, that I turned on the TV and watched the premier episode of *Saturday Night Live*. "Fuck," I thought, "they did it." The new comedy had been brought to the airwaves in New York by people I didn't know, and they were incredibly good at it, too. The show was a heavy blow to my inner belief that I alone was leading the cavalry and carrying the new comedy flag. *Saturday Night Live* and I, however, were destined to meet.

My performing roll continued. Dave Felton, a highly regarded rock-and-roll journalist, interviewed me for an article in *Rolling Stone*. He did a perceptive job of quoting my act verbatim, using pauses, italics, and sudden jumps into all capital letters. It read funny, even the visual stuff, and rather than kill the act through exposure, he made it a necessity to see in person. Felton wrote, "This isn't comedy; it's campfire recreation for the bent at heart. It's a laugh-along for loonies. Disneyland on acid." On the strength of everything that was happening, Bill McEuen closed a record deal with an uneasy Warner Bros. He took the Boarding House recordings up to his studio in Aspen and began editing them.

I was still adding to the show. My Ramblin' Guy persona had been inspired, way back, by the folksinger Ramblin' Jack Elliott's outlaw stance, then reinforced by the Allman Brothers' hit "Ramblin' Man" and even Joni

Mitchell's "He's a rambler and a gambler and a sweet-talkin' ladies man." It seemed like all the sexy guys were ramblers! I would sing: "I'M RA-uh-AM-uh-AM-uh-AM . . . [long pause] . . . BLIN'!" I liked to give myself heroic qualities that were obviously delusional. I started saying with mock self-importance, "I'm so wild." Then "I'm a wild and crazy guy." Which actually was a bailout if a bit didn't work. The piece developed into this: "Yes . . . I am . . . a wild and craaaazy guy . . . the kind of guy who might like to do annnaything . . . at any time . . . to drink champagne at three A.M. or maybe . . . at four A.M. . . . eat a live chipmunk . . . or maybe even . . . [excitedly] . . . WEAR TWO SOCKS ON ONE FOOT."

Forces converged. The article in *Rolling Stone,* my live performances, appearances on *The Tonight Show,* a modestly produced one-man show on the new and experimental network HBO, and intriguing reviews and press made audiences ignite. The confluence that I had doubted would ever happen through auditions for sitcoms was now happening outside of Hollywood's control. My audience was developing more like a rock-and-roll band's than a comedian's: I was underground and on the road.

Outside of the big cities, I was playing concerts seating about five hundred people, a small number, but they were avid. Aggressive fans, sometimes wearing arrows through their heads or balloon hats, were gathering outside the stage door after the shows, and I had to have a guard walk me safely to my car. After a show at a college in Boise,

Idaho, I said to the two student escorts, "Stand close, I'll sign a few autographs, but we should keep moving toward the car." I pushed open the stage door. A rush of Idaho silence. Nobody. Nothing but twinkling stars. Idaho hadn't gotten the word yet. The two students looked at me with disgust.

Some promoters got on board and booked me into a theater in Dallas. Before the show I asked one of them, "How many people are out there?" "Two thousand," he said. Two thousand? How could there be two thousand? That night I did my usual bit of taking people outside, but it was starting to get dangerous and difficult. First, people were standing in the streets, where they could be hit by a car. Second, only a small number of the audience could hear or see me (could Charlton Heston really have been audible when he was addressing a thousand extras?). Third, it didn't seem as funny or direct with so many people; I reluctantly dropped it from my repertoire.

I now had the luxury of performing only one show per night, which meant that after a dozen years of two, three, and even five shows per day, I no longer had to include a weak bit in order to fill time. I cut lines that I loved but which rarely worked, such as:

"I think communication is so firsbern."

Or:

"I'm so depressed today. I just found out this 'death thing' applies to me."

And:

"I have no fear, no fear at all. I wake up, and I have no fear. I go to bed without fear. Fear, fear, fear, fear. Yes, 'fear' is a word that is not in my vocabulary."

Or this weird one:

"I just found out I'm vain. I thought that song was about me."

I continued doing *The Tonight Show* and performing in concert. Before a show in Milwaukee, I asked the promoter, "How many are out there?" Three thousand. Three thousand? It didn't seem possible. I worried about being seen at such distances—this was a small comedy act. For visibility, I bought a white suit to wear onstage. I was conflicted because the white suit had already been used by entertainers, including John Lennon. I was afraid it might seem derivative, but I stayed with it for practical reasons, and it didn't seem to matter to the audience or critics. The suit was made of gabardine, which always stayed fresh and flowed smoothly with my body. It got noticed in the press because it was three-piece, which appeared to be a symbol of conservatism, but I really wore the vest so my shirt would stay tucked into my pants. How could I "look better than they do" if my shirt was blousing out between my belt and my suit button? I was now coming up with jokes about the increased size of the house. My opening was the magic dime trick, in which I would claim to change the date of a dime. Then I would ask the back row what they'd paid to get in. They would shout it out, and I would laugh hysterically, implying that they were getting screwed.

Lorne Michaels, the producer of *SNL*, inquired about my hosting the show. Yes and yes, I said. I flew to New York a few days early, and Lorne walked me into the busy studio on Saturday afternoon. Gilda Radner's cheery lilt and Laraine Newman's alto voice crisscrossed as they rehearsed a sketch. Chevy Chase noodled on a piano in a corner. Danny Aykroyd and John Belushi, one a virtuoso and one a hurricane, energetically entertained each other while the cameras swung around the studio, and the dominant sound was the resonance of Danny's big laugh. Belushi turned out to be the nicest rowdy person I ever met. Both scary and down-to-earth, he once told me, "I never yell at the staff, only the department heads."

In Lorne's office later that day, the leather-clad Danny Aykroyd told me he had been up all night riding his motorcycle, and when it had stalled at four A.M., he had thumbed a ride. When the car got up to speed, the driver pushed him out of the moving vehicle, and he rolled onto the rainy streets of Manhattan. I pictured Danny bouncing down the wet pavement and then said the only thing that came to mind. I asked him if he wanted to go to Saks and shop for clothes. He said, as friendly as he could, "Uh, man, that's not my thing." We liked each other, but we were different.

I first appeared on *Saturday Night Live* in October 1976. I felt powerful butterflies just prior to being introduced, especially when I reminded myself that it was live, and anything that went wrong stayed wrong. But it is possible to will confidence. My consistent performing schedule had kept me sharp; it would have been difficult to blow it. I did two monologues straight out of my act; some sketches, including *Jeopardy! 1999* (remember, this was 1976); and a spoof commercial where I pitched a dog that was also a watch, called Fido-Flex. The show turned out well, though I didn't realize how well. The next Monday I had a concert in Madison, Wisconsin. It would be my first show after the *SNL* appearance. "How many are out there?" I asked. Six thousand. Six thousand? At least twice the normal. I walked onstage and was greeted with a roar of such intensity that I remember feeling both pleasure and fear. In response to the deafening approval, I was, like an athlete at the college play-offs, flooded with adrenaline. I made quick adjustments for the thundering cheers and the increased audience size. I bore down. My physicality intensified and compressed—smaller gestures had greater meaning—and my comedy became more potent as I settled deeper into my own body. I opened the show with this line: "I have decided to give the greatest performance of my life! Oh, wait, sorry, that's tomorrow night."

My fame knocked on my parents' door. They couldn't help hearing about their son. My father, though, was not impressed. After my first appearance on *Saturday Night Live*, he wrote a bad review of me in his newsletter for the Newport Beach Association of Realtors, of which he was president: "His performance did nothing to further his career." Later, shamefaced, my father told me that his best friend had come into his office holding the newsletter, placed it on his desk, and shaken his head sternly, indicating a wordless "This is wrong." I believe my father didn't like what I was doing in my work and was embarrassed by it. Perhaps he thought his friends were embarrassed by it, too, and the review was to indicate that he was not sanctioning this new comedy. Later, he gave an interview in a newspaper in which he said, "I think *Saturday Night Live* is the most horrible thing on television." I suppressed anything I felt about his comments because I couldn't let him have power over my work. After all, I explained to myself, the whole point of this comedy was to turn off the older crowd while reeling in the young. But as my career progressed, I noticed that my father remained uncomplimentary toward my comedy, and what I did about it still makes sense to me: I never discussed my work with him again.

But my mother was aglow. She had a continuing fascination with celebrities, and now she had one of her own. She was never moved by *what* I was doing (in an interview she said, "He writes his own material, I'm always telling him he needs a new writer"), but she was very involved with *how* things were going. She kept up with every little appearance and success and reported anything positive her friends had said to her, though sometimes she couldn't discern the fine line between a compliment and an insult. After I'd started making films, she once told me, "Oh, my friends went to the movies last weekend, and they couldn't get in anywhere so they went to see yours, and they loved it!"

I was a newly minted star when we were driving through Beverly Hills and she said, "Get out and walk down the street so I can watch people look at you." I gently declined, explaining to her how uncomfortable it would make me feel, but it never sank in. Another time she said, "I was in line at the supermarket yesterday, and when they found out I was your mother . . . !" I keep puzzling over the exact phraseology my proud mama must have used to work her information into normal supermarket discourse.

Money trickled her way—I was able to give her a monthly clothes allowance—and she was ecstatic. She became a regular at Neiman Marcus and loved that she was modestly famous as she browsed the racks of her favorite designer, St. John. When our mother died, my sister, Melinda, had an idea. She suggested our mother be buried on a hillside, in a plot overlooking the upscale Fashion Island shopping center in Orange County. And that is exactly what we did.

My first album, *Let's Get Small*, released in 1977, sold a million and a half copies. The material was so vivid to Bill and me that we naively included bits that were largely visual. The uninitiated heard clanks and spaces that brought forth laughs, and this minus turned into a plus, as the transitions seemed more surreal than they already were. Audiences were intrigued to see live what they could only hear on the album, and the theaters filled.

During my third appearance on *Saturday Night Live* I incorporated a line from my act, "I'm a wild and crazy guy," into Danny Aykroyd's idea (along with Marilyn Miller and James Downey) about two Czechoslovakian brothers. We caught the public's fancy, which gave me my second ticket into catchphrase heaven. My second album, *A Wild and Crazy Guy*, released in 1978, was being

Danny Aykroyd and me as the Czech brothers.

promoted every time we did the sketch on the show. It sold two and a half million copies and went to number one on the charts. Well, okay, number two. Promotion was becoming a regular part of the job, and when I did *The Tonight Show* it was understood that either I or Johnny would hold up an album for all to see. After *A Wild and Crazy Guy* blistered the record charts in 1978, I was on the cover of *Rolling Stone* and *Newsweek*.

I hadn't significantly collaborated with other performers since my days at the Bird Cage. My appearances on *SNL*, whether I was dancing with Gilda Radner, clowning with Danny, pitching show ideas with Lorne and the writers, or simply admiring Bill Murray, were community comic efforts that made me feel like I had been dropped off at a playground rather than the office. Watching the gleam in your partner's eyes, acting on impulses that had been nurtured over thousands of shows, working with edgy comic actors—some so edgy they died from it—was thrilling. We were all united in one, single goal, which was, using the comedian's parlance, to kill.

The record sales and the appearances on *SNL* compounded the size of the live audience. How many tickets sold? I asked in Toronto. "Fifteen thousand," they said. In St. Louis, I was told, "Twenty-two thousand." The act was on fire. My set lists from the period, now tattered and yellowed, remind me of forgotten routines: I would sing "I Can See Clearly Now" and walk into the mike. I would juggle kittens (swapping the one real kitten for a stuffed look-alike); I would stand in spilled water and touch the mike, faking an electric shock, then do it again as though I had enjoyed it. I had a long routine (for me) in which I confessed my weird sexual fetish, "I like to wear men's underwear."

There were more:

"I know what you're thinking," I would say conspiratorially, "you're thinking, 'Steve, how can you be so fuckin' funny?'"

In my opening seconds, I would say, "It's great to be here," then move to several other spots on the stage and say, "No, it's great to be here!" I would move again: "No, it's great to be here!"

Shouting to the audience, "Everybody put your hands together!" I would put my hands together and hold them there, making only one clap, saying, "Now keep them together!"

"Hello, Crime Stoppers! [audience: "Hello, Steve."] Let's repeat the Crime Stoppers' oath: 'I promise not to depreciate items carried forward from one tax year as nondepreciable items!'"

"I've learned in comedy never to alienate the audience. Otherwise, I would be like Dimitri in *La Condition Humaine*. . . ."

"A lot of people wonder if Steve Martin is my real name. Well, I did change my name for show business. My real name is Gern Blanston. So please, just call me . . . [long pause] . . . Gern." Don't ask me why, but this was funny at the time. There is even a Gern Blanston website, and for a while there was a rock band that used the name.

"I'm so mad at my mother, she's a hundred and two years old, and she called me the other day. She wanted to borrow *ten dollars for some food!* I said, 'Hey, I work for a living!'"

I would stand onstage and tune my banjo, but my hand would be about a foot away from the tuners, twisting in the air. I would act as though I couldn't figure out why it wouldn't go in tune.

And my closer, "Well, we've had a good time tonight, considering we're all going to die someday."

Moovin' and groovin' onstage.

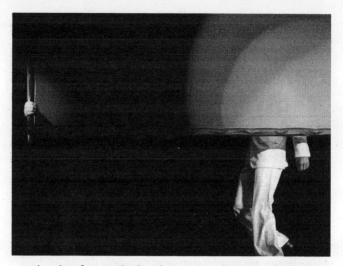

I loved performing this bit. There was a movie screen onstage, and I would go behind it and attach a fake rubber hand to it as though the hand were mine. Then I would slowly move backward, making it appear as if my arm was stretching.

IN THE LATE SEVENTIES, I continued to tour. My schedule was this: After sleeping all night on a band bus, I would arrive at the hotel around seven A.M. and collapse in a groggy half-sleep until four P.M. Then I would have a room-service dinner, and the only thing on the hotel menu that fit my fish-a-tarian diet was breaded fried shrimp with the texture of sandpaper, really just a ketchup delivery system. Following that, I would dumbly watch the five-thirty P.M. airing of *The Brady Bunch* (this showing, it seemed, was universal), then I would do the show. We—my roadie, Maple, and the sound team— were moving with such clockwork that some nights it

178

Date	CITY	Time	Hotel	TRANSPORTATION	FACILITY	Remarks
SEP. 8 fri.	FRESNO CA	7:30 & 10:30	Smugglers Inn 209-226-2200	lv Airresearch 4:34 (LADY AVIA.) 5:00 lv Beechcraft Wst arr Airresearch 1:46	CAL. ST. UNIV. Amphitheatre	2 SHOWS (catering) LEAR: LADY AVIATION @ 5 yrs. drive from L.A.
9- sat. thru' 17 su.	UNIVERSAL CITY CA	8:15 nightly			Universal Amphitheatre	w. Blues Bros. maple: Trop. 213-652-5720
25 mon.	Burbank Ca.	5:30		—26th tue:— LAX-LAS 7:15-8:05, WA#232	NBC The Tonight Show	
27 wed.	SALT LAKE CITY UT	7:00 & 10:00	Hotel Utah 801-531-1000	LAS-SLC 10:30-12:34 WA #406	(UNIV. of UTAH) Special Event Center	2 SHOWS (MOUNTAIN TIME)
28 thu. 29 fri.	CHICAGO IL	7:30 & 10:30	Ritz-Carlton 312-266-1000	SLC-ORD 9:40-1:25 UA #276	International Amphitheatre	2 SHOWS (FRIDAY) DORAINE FRI 9:45am (CENTRAL TIME)
30 sat.	KANSAS CITY MO.	8:00	Crown Centre 816-474-4400	ORD-MCI 12:00-1:16 TW #163	Kemper Arena	
OCT. 1 sun.	ST. PAUL MN.	7:30	Radisson 612-222-7711	MCI-MSP 11:10-12:15 BN# 124	Civic Center Arena	
2 mon.	LEXINGTON KY.	8:00	Hyatt Regency 606-233-4111	MSP-ORD 1035-11:30 NW# 436 ORD-LEX 1:11-2:09 DL# 145	Lex. Center Arena	meet bus: overnight to Greensboro (eastern time)
3 tue.	GREENSBORO NC.	8:00	Howard Johnson's (Coliseum) 919-294-4920	overnights	Coliseum Arena	
4 wed.	PITTSBURG PA.	8:00	Hyatt House (Chatham Center) 412-391-5000		Civic Arena	
5 thu.	COLLEGE PARK MD.	7:30	Madison (Washington d.c.) 202-785-1000	≈5hr.	(UNIV. OF MD.) Cole Fieldhouse	crew: Sheraton N.E. 301-459-6700
6 fri. 7 sat.	UNIONDALE NY.	7:30 & 10:30	Carlyle (NYc) 212-744-1600	≈5hr. overnight	Nassau Veteran's Mem. Coliseum	crew: 2 Shows Holiday Inn FRI Hemp Stead 516-496-4100
8 sat. 9 sun.	BOSTON MS.	7:30 & 10:30	Hyatt (Cambridge) 617-492-1234	≈5hr.	John B. Hynes Veteran's Auditorium	2 Show sun. mon: 3 SHOWS 4:00-7:30-10:30
10	NEW HAVEN	8:00	Sheraton Plaza	≈2hr.	veteran's mem. Coliseum	

One month's itinerary; design by Maple Byrne. Even though it indicates two shows at the Nassau Coliseum, a third was added. I remember nothing on this schedule except the Universal Amphitheatre—because it was in my hometown and opening the show were my friends the Blues Brothers—and the Nassau Coliseum, because of the harrowing helicopter ride to get from Manhattan to Long Island, with jets from LaGuardia Airport streaking all around us.

seemed as though we were rolling down the highway for the next town before the applause had stopped in the arena.

Sixty cities in sixty-three days. Seventy-two cities in eighty days. Eighty-five cities in ninety days. The Coliseum in Richfield, Ohio, largest audience in one day, 18,695. The Chicago International Amphitheatre: twenty-nine thousand people. Stealth limousines and subterranean entrances. I played Nassau Coliseum in New York. How many tickets sold? Forty-five thousand. I was astonished that popular culture had fixed its attention so intensely on my little act. This lightning strike was happening to me, Stephen Glenn Martin, who had started from zero, from a magic act, from juggling in my backyard, from Disneyland, from the Bird Cage, and I was now the biggest concert comedian in show business, ever. I was elated. My success had outstripped my wildest aspirations. I had hit a gusher, and I stopped checking prices in restaurants, hotels, and clothing stores. I bought my first house, and then I bought my second house, skillfully negotiated by my father. My wisecrack about success was "We'll offer you fifty thousand dollars to go stand over there." "I can't," I would say, "I'm getting seventy-five thousand to stand right here." I had a line: "I think I'm spending my money wisely. . . . I just bought a three-hundred-dollar pair of socks. And last week I got a gasoline-powered turtleneck sweater."

Standing Down

THE ACT WAS SHIFTING into automatic. The choreography was in place, and all I had to do was fulfill it. I was performing a litany of immediate old favorites, and the laughs, rather than being the result of spontaneous combustion, now seemed to roll in like waves created far out at sea. The nuances of stand-up still thrilled me, but nuance was difficult when you were a white dot in a basketball arena. This was no longer an experiment; I felt a huge responsibility not to let people down. Arenas of twenty thousand and three-day gigs of forty-five thousand were no place to try out new material. I dabbled with changes, introducing a small addition or mutation here and there, but they were swallowed up by the echoing, cavernous venues.

Onstage, Syracuse, New York, 1978, as King Tut.

STEVE MARTIN

Though the audiences continued to grow, I experienced a concomitant depression caused by exhaustion, isolation, and creative ennui. As I was too famous to go outdoors without a discomforting hoopla, my romantic interludes ceased because I no longer had normal access to civilized life. The hour and a half I spent performing was still fun, but there were no band members, no others onstage, and after the show, I took a solitary ride back to the hotel, where I was speedily escorted by security across the lobby. A key went in a door, and boom: the blunt interior of a hotel room. Nowhere to look but inward. I'm sure there were a hundred solutions. I could have invited friends to join me on the road, or asked a feel-good guru to shake my shoulders and say, "Perk up, you idiot," but I was too exhausted to communicate, and it seemed like a near-coma was the best way to spend the day. This was, as the cliché goes, the loneliest period of my life.

I was caught and I could not quit, because this multizeroed income might last only a moment. I couldn't imagine abandoning something I had worked so hard to craft. I knew about the flash in the pan, I had seen it happen to others, and I worried about it happening to me. In the middle of all this, I saw that the only way I could go, at best, was sideways. I wasn't singing songs that you hum forever; I was doing comedy, which is as ephemeral as the daily newspaper. Onstage I was no longer the funniest I ever was; my shelf life was expiring. I recently found a discarded joke among my papers: "You might think I'm making a lot of money, but you have to understand my expenses. Twenty percent to a manager, ten percent to an agent, thirty percent to travel, and .000000005 percent to develop new material." It was 1979, and I was already booked for the next two years.

The prospect of the remaining stand-up dates loomed over me. The glowing reviews changed; I was now a target. Critics who once lauded me were starting to rebel. Easy headlines appeared: STEVE MARTIN, A MILD AND LAZY GUY. I received a bad review in a local newspaper before I even performed. The backlash had begun. My tired body had rebelled, too. One summer night I was midway through my show in a southern college gymnasium when the temperature reached 120. In a resurrection of my old anxiety, my heart began to skip beats, and I panicked. I abruptly walked offstage and went to a hospital, where I was given a well-attended celebrity EKG. Fine. Stress and heat, I was told, but as I was lying on a gurney, with the sheet up to my neck but not quite over my head, confident that I was dying, a nurse asked me to autograph the printout of my erratic heartbeat. I perfunctorily signed to avoid further stress. The concept of privacy crystallized at that moment and became something to protect. What I was doing, what I was thinking, and who I was seeing, I now kept to myself as a necessary defense against the feeling that I was becoming, like the Weinermobile, a commercial artifact. Once, in Texas, a woman came up to me and said, with some humor and a lot of drawl, "Are you that Steve Martin thang?"

Being the good Baptist-raised boy I was, I honored all my contracts and did the shows, though with mounting frustration. The act was still rocking, but audience disruptions, whoops and shouts, sometimes killed the timing of bits, violating my premise that *every moment mattered*. The days of the heckler comebacks were over. The audiences were so large that if someone was calling or signaling to me, only I and their immediate seatmates could hear them. My timing was jarred, yet if I had responded to the heckler, the rest of the audience wouldn't have known what I was talking about. Today I realize that I misunderstood what my last year of stand-up was about. I had become a party host, presiding not over timing and ideas but over a celebratory bash of my own making. If I had understood what was happening, I might have been happier, but I didn't. I still thought I was doing comedy.

During this time, I asked a woman to dinner, and she accepted. After the salad course, she started talking about her boyfriend.

"You have a boyfriend?" I asked, puzzled.

"Yes, I do."

"Does he know you're out with me?" I asked.

"Yes, he does."

"And what does he think of that?"

"He thinks it's great!"

I was now famous, and the normal rules of social interaction no longer applied.

Suddenly, restaurant reservations were always available, and VIP considerations made hassles with travel, long lines, and rude salesclerks vanish. Waiters were cordial and prompt. Every call was returned, there was no further need for ID, and I was able to meet artists whom I admired. I was surprised by James Cagney's noblesse oblige phone call to my New York hotel room just to say hello, and by Cary Grant's friendly backstage chat at the American Film Institute's salute to Gene Kelly, during which he seriously charmed my girlfriend.

But guess what. There was a dark side. A regular conversation, except with established friends, became difficult, fraught with ulterior motives, and often degenerated into deadening nephew autograph requests. Almost every ordinary action that took place in public had a freakish celebrity aura around it. I would get laughs at innocuous things I said, such as "What time does the movie start?" or "Hello." I would pull my hat down low on my head and stare at the ground when I walked through airports, and I would duck around corners quickly at museums. My room-service meal could be delivered by four people wearing arrows through their heads—funny, yes, but when you're dead tired of your own jokes, it's hard to respond with the expected glee. Cars would follow me recklessly on the freeway, and I worried for the passengers' lives as the driver hung out the window, shouting, "I'm a wild and craaaazzzzyy guy!" while steering with one hand and holding a beer in the other. In a public situation, I was expected to be the figure I was onstage, which I stubbornly resisted. People were waiting for a show, but my show was only that, a show. It was precise and particular and not reproducible in a living room; in fact, to me my act was serious.

Fame suited me in that the icebreaking was already done and my natural shyness could be easily overcome. I was, however, ill suited for fame's destruction of privacy, for the uninvited doorbell ringers and anonymous phone callers. I had never been outgoing, and when strangers approached me with the familiarity of old friends, I felt dishonest if I returned it in kind.

When I got divorced in 1992, a tabloid reported that I would practice my routines in front of a mirror, and if they weren't going well, I would find my wife and scream at her. At the time, as I was naturally sensitive about the divorce, this lie seemed almost actionable. And once, on a local Los Angeles news show dealing with "celebrity assassinations," I was shown getting out of a car while crosshairs were superimposed over my head along with the sound effect of a rifle crack. In spite of these examples, I have been treated fairly for most of my career in showbiz, probably by being dull and dreary and failing to excite the needle on the gossipometer. I admit that I'm a lousy interview. My magician's instincts make me reluctant to tell 'em how it's done, whether it's a movie, book, play, or any aspect of personal life. Sometimes a journalist will lean in and say, "You're very private." And I mentally respond,

187

"Someone who's private would not be doing an interview on television."

Time has helped me achieve peace with celebrity. At first I was not famous enough, then I was too famous, now I am famous just right. Oh yes, I have heard the argument that celebrities want fame when it's useful and don't when it's not. That argument is absolutely true.

I WAS DETERMINED to parlay my stand-up success into motion pictures while I still had some clout. A movie career seemed to foster longevity, whereas a career as a comedian who had become a fad seemed finite. Plus, the travel was exhausting me, and I swooned at the idea that instead of my going to every town to perform my act, a movie would go while I stayed home.

I had an idea for a film. It came from a line in my act: "It wasn't always easy for me; I was born a poor black child." That was the idea, and that was all I had. I knew only that I wanted the movie to have the feel of a saga, and I toyed with story ideas.

I was hot enough to get in any door, or so I thought. Bill McEuen had a relationship with David Picker, then the head of Paramount Pictures. This was not a time when it was automatic that a popular comedian could land a movie deal, so the prospect was considered carefully by the studio. I gave them the notes on a screenplay I had dabbled with.

We see Steve sitting on the porch of a ramshackle
tenement farm in Tennessee. He is his white self while
his black family members do chores about the yard. His
mother, a big black woman à la Hattie McDaniel, sits
on the porch and sings the blues. Steve says things like
"Gosh, Mom, that's really great blues you're singing!"
His family relationship is very close with his black brothers
and sisters, so when he makes a decision to go on the road
after hearing the music of Lawrence Welk on the radio, it
is a sad occasion. There is a tearful farewell, and Steve sets
off hitchhiking in the front of the family house and gets a
ride about two hours later. His family stands outside with
him in awkward silence while he waits for a ride.

The notes continue to describe a series of odd jobs that
"Steve" gets on his journey: a ranch hand who practices
roping fence posts and ends up with a herd of fence posts;
a buffalo counter in Beverly Hills who stands on Rodeo
Drive—after several days, a buffalo finally walks by, and
"Steve" takes out a clipboard and writes down, "One." My
list of odd jobs went on: "My third job, perhaps the weird-
est of all, was standing on my head in a river." None of
these odd jobs ended up in the movie, which was ulti-
mately written and rewritten many times with Carl Gott-
lieb and Michael Elias. Eventually, Bill McEuen and David
Picker, who by now had left the studio, moved the film to
Universal after Paramount passed.

Carl Reiner, who, in a six-year burst of comic perfec-

189

tion, wrote and produced television's *The Dick Van Dyke Show*, was our lucky choice as director. Carl and I met constantly. His memory was sharp as cheddar, and he would spontaneously relate anecdotes relevant to our work. One day I mentioned concern over my lack of concrete talents. Carl told me about his first appearance on *The Sid Caesar Show*, a sketch in which he spoke a long stretch of German-sounding gibberish. The next day his mother called and said, "Carl, I was with some ladies in the park, and they said they didn't know you spoke German." Carl said, "Ma, that's why they hire me, because I *can't* speak German." Carl's mother then said, "Well, the ladies don't have to know that."

We were still mulling over titles for the movie. One day I said to Carl, "It needs to be something short, yet have the feeling of an epic tale. Like Dostoyevsky's *The Idiot*, but not that. Like *The Jerk*." The title, after a few more days of analyzing, stuck.

I was injecting stage material into the screenplay, including a bit that was taken directly from the end of my act, first developed at the Boarding House. Onstage, I would exit through the audience, saying, "I'm quitting, I'm leaving and never coming back, and I don't need anything, nothing at all, well, I need this ashtray." I would collect doodads from the tabletops until I finally disappeared out the door. The bit appears in the final film as I forlornly leave Bernadette Peters and my movie mansion:

"Well, I'm gonna go then! And I don't need any of this! I don't need this stuff [*I push all of the letters off the desk*], and I don't need you. I don't need anything except this [*I pick up an ashtray*], and that's it and that's the only thing I need, is this. Just this ashtray. And this paddle game, the ashtray and the paddle game and that's all I need. And this remote control. The ashtray, the paddle game and the remote control, and that's all I need. And these matches. The ashtray, and these matches, and the remote control and the paddle ball. And this lamp. The ashtray, this paddle game and the remote control and the lamp and that's all I need. I don't need one other thing, not one—I need this! [*I pick up a magazine.*] The paddle game, the remote control, and the matches, for sure. And this! [*I pick up a chair.*] And that's all I need. The ashtray, the remote control, the paddle game, this magazine, and the chair. Well, what are you looking at? What do you think I am, some kind of a jerk or something?"

It was a joy to work on the movie and the script. Our goal in writing was a laugh on every page. But my favorite line in the movie was an ad lib, one that is mildly obscured by traffic noise in the finished film. My character, Navin Johnson, is hitchhiking in Missouri, headed for the big city. A car pulls over, and the driver asks, "St. Louis?" "No," I answer, "Navin Johnson."

We made the film and went off to preview it in St. Louis. As much as I loved the comedy in the movie, my favorite moment was when Bernadette Peters and I sang a simple song on a beach, "Tonight You Belong to Me," a tune that was a hit in the twenties and again in the fifties, when it was recorded by two adolescent sisters called Patience and Prudence. I thought the scene was touching, and I couldn't wait for it to come on-screen, hoping the audience would be as affected as I had been. The movie was rolling along with lots of laughter. Then the song came on. Mass exodus for popcorn. Song over, audience returned for more laughs. After the screening, I got a left-handed compliment of juicy perfection: A woman approached me and said, "I *loved* this movie. And my husband loved it, and he hates you!"

The world of moviemaking had changed me. Carl Reiner ran a joyful set. Movies were social; stand-up was antisocial. I was not judged every day by a changing audience. It was fun to have lunches with cast and crew and to dream up material in the morning that could be shot seven different ways in the afternoon and evaluated—and possibly perfected—in the editing room months later. The end of a movie is like graduation day, and right or wrong, we felt we had accomplished something wonderful. I got another benefit: my daily observation of Carl Reiner. He had an entrenched sense of glee; he used humor as a gentle way of speaking difficult truths; and he could be effortlessly frank. He taught me more about how to be a social person than any other adult in my life.

The Jerk, receiving one lone good review from a small

paper in Florida and getting dismissive and sadistic reviews from the rest of the country, made one hundred eighty million dollars in old money. It was recently voted among the American Film Institute's top one hundred comedies of all time, he said smugly. Because it was a hit, my life changed, though again, my father was not impressed. I had invited him to the premiere. The Bruin Theatre in Westwood, next to UCLA, was ringed outside with spotlights drawing figure eights in the sky and packed inside with clamoring, vocal fans. Press crews lined the red carpet, and it took us forty-five minutes to get from the car to our seats. The movie played well, and afterward my friends and I took my father to dinner at a quiet, old-fashioned eatery that didn't offer "silly" modern food. He said nothing about the film; he talked about everything but the film. Finally, one of my friends said, "Glenn, what did you think of Steve's movie?" My father chuckled and said, "Well, he's no Charlie Chaplin."

My body was on the road but my heart was elsewhere. I continued to fulfill my contracts, mostly weekly gigs where I was allowed to "sit down," a term meaning the performer wasn't having to travel to a different town every night. Working in Vegas for several weeks, I taped tinfoil over the windows in my rental house so I could adjust to the city's all-night schedule. According to scientists, no sunlight for two weeks can do things to a person, such as make you insane. I fell into a depression that might be called self-indulgent but was real just the same.

193
—

The Jerk had been a smash hit, but my comic well was dry; the movie represented my small act's ultimate expression. My cheap cassette player, which I now used to play thirties songs from *Pennies from Heaven*—the dark, audience-jolting drama that I chose to do next—was my only solace inside the blacked-out bedroom.

In 1981 my act was like an overly plumed bird whose next evolutionary step was extinction. One night in Las Vegas, I saw something so disturbing that I didn't mention it to my friends, my agent, or my manager. It was received in my mind like grim, inevitable news. I was onstage at the Riviera showroom, and the house, as usual, was full. The floor tables were jammed, and the club was ringed with tiers of booths. There were soft lights around the interior wall, which silhouetted the patrons in halos of light. My eyes scanned the room as I worked, seeing heads bobbing and nodding; and then, in one booth in the back, I saw something I hadn't seen in five years: empty seats. I had reached the top of the roller coaster.

I had a week's job in Atlantic City. The shows were still sold out, but I was exhausted, physically and existentially. When I performed the song "King Tut," a guitar suspended on wires (a beautiful, mirrored Fender Flying-V) would descend from the rafters. I would then "Tut walk" over and strum it only once, and it would ascend back into the ceiling, creating the shortest guitar solo in the history of show business. For the third night in a row, the guitar failed to descend, leaving me horribly stuck. I guessed that I hadn't greased the right union guy. The act ended normally, and I exited the stage and felt something rare for me: rage. In the wings, I began swearing to myself. I ripped off my coat and threw it against a wall. Of course, my fury was not from the failure of the King Tut guitar to descend from the ceiling— it was that over the last few years I had lost contact with what I was doing, and I was suffering an artistic crisis that I didn't know I had a capacity for. I went to my dressing room, opened my travel-weary black prop case, and stowed away my magic act, thinking that one day I would open it and look at it sentimentally, which for no particular reason, I haven't. I never did stand-up again.

IN THE EARLY 1980s, a friend whose father had been killed crossing the street and whose mother had committed suicide on Mother's Day advised me, "If you have anything to work out with your parents, do it now. One day it will be too late." This thought nagged at me and I began a fifteen-year effort to reconnect with my parents. I took them to lunch almost every weekend, probing them for anecdotes about our life together, and these consistent visits made us closer. My father enjoyed dealing with fan-mail requests and used his real estate expertise to help manage my vacation home. In the 1990s, my father's attitude toward me began to soften. I had written *Picasso at the Lapin Agile*, a play set in 1905 about a hypothetical meeting between Picasso and Einstein. My father flipped over it, bragging to his friends and telling me I should win a Pulitzer Prize. He was laughing more, too, enjoying pranks on telemarketers and mail solicitors, and he exhibited his charitable streak by delivering Meals on Wheels, a service that provides food to the elderly. I began to appreciate him more as his humor started to shine through. Though he was experiencing disturbing health issues, he took my twenty-five-year-old nephew, Rusty, to a car dealer to help him negotiate a price. After a few offers and counteroffers, the dealer looked at the purchase order and said, "I don't know, I'm not really comfortable with this."

"You're uncomfortable? You're uncomfortable?" my father said. "I'm the one with the catheter in my peter."

After our lunches, my parents, now in their eighties, would walk me to my car. I would kiss my mother on the cheek and wave awkwardly at my father as we said good-bye. But one afternoon, perhaps motivated by a vague awareness that time was running out, we hugged each other and he said, in a voice barely audible, "I love you." This would be the first time these words were ever spoken between us. Several days later, I sent him a letter that began, "I heard what you said," and I wrote the same words back to him.

My father's health declined further, and he became bedridden. There must be an instinct about when the end

196

is near; Melinda and I found ourselves at our parents' home in Laguna Beach, California. I walked into the house they had lived in for thirty-five years, and my tearful sister said, "He's saying goodbye to everyone." A nurse said to me, "This is when it all happens." I didn't know what she meant, but I soon understood.

I was alone with him in the bedroom; his mind was alert but his body was failing. He said, almost buoyantly, "I'm ready now." I sat on the edge of the bed, and another silence fell over us. Then he said, "I wish I could cry, I wish I could cry."

At first I took this as a comment on his condition but am forever thankful that I pushed on. "What do you want to cry about?" I said.

"For all the love I received and couldn't return."

I felt a chill of familiarity.

There was another lengthy silence as we looked into each other's eyes. At last he said, "You did everything I wanted to do."

"I did it for you," I said. Then we wept for the lost years. I was glad I didn't say the more complicated truth: "I did it *because* of you."

Our father's sickness reunited me and my sister. When we visited our ailing parents, we did something we had never done in our lives: talked. We had something uniquely in common, and each conversation turned to our past, as though we had found a mine with a rich vein. I was surprised that our views of the household jibed. I had thought I was the only outsider, but no, she was, too. She was aware of the tension and fear that had made home life so miserable and the outside world so appealing. When she confirmed our father's unprovoked hostility toward me, I was shocked. Somehow I thought I had made it up, had caused it, or had an innate, unlikable quality that riled him.

Together again.

STEVE MARTIN

My father died in 1997, and my mother, for a short time, became a stylish matriarch. She immediately cut off all the consistent small loans my father had continued to make to a few friends; to her they were freeloaders. But she didn't have long to enjoy her single life. Having few interests to sustain her, over the next few years she fell into a vacant, mental decline. I continued my visits with her, and always when I walked into the room, her blue eyes lit up and her face brought forth a smile. I was, after all, her son.

She began to alternate between lucidity and confusion, creating moments of tenderness and painful hilarity. She told me she thought Glenn had treated me unfairly, that she wished she had intervened. She said when I was a child, she hugged me and kissed me a lot, something I did not recollect. Then she took a long pause. She looked at me, quietly puzzled, and said, "How's your mother?"

Another day, curious about an old family rumor, I asked her if she ever had a miscarriage. "No, I never did." Then my ninety-year-old mother added, "Knock on wood."

One emotional afternoon I told her that I loved her and I thanked her for bringing me into the world. Her eyes moistened, and she said, "This is the highest moment of my life." I asked her if she had any regrets. She said, "I wish I had been more truthful," a comment regarding, I believe, her lifelong subordination to my father. She expressed embarrassment that she was dying, saying, "I hate to be silly." In February 2002 she lay on a bed in the

199

house, not able to speak, but with her eyes smiling. Her saintly Filipino nurse, Mila, was daubing her head with a damp towel and was, in an eerie recall from my childhood, singing to her "America the Beautiful." Then Mila quietly left the room. I moved closer and said goodbye to my mother. I put my arms around her and, surprising myself, choked out, "Mama, Mama, Mama," a term I hadn't used since childhood. I kissed her on the cheek, and her skin felt cool and young. She seemed to pass into a trance, and eventually, I left the house.

I drove toward home and on the way felt a sentimental urge to stop by the Bird Cage. It had been thirty-one years since I had left the little theater where I got my start. I cruised the main gate, but the lines were long. I almost went home but decided to try the employee entrance in the back. I pulled in to a parking space wondering if they were going to throw me out, but an elderly security guard immediately said, "Hi, Steve." He was saying hello to me not as a celebrity but as someone he remembered from thirty years ago. A few hand waves were telegraphed from security guard to security guard, and I found myself entering the grounds through the employees' gate.

Knott's had expanded over the decades, giving it the qualities of a tree trunk: The newest developments were on the outside, with the oldest buildings still standing at its core. As I moved toward the theater, I felt a peculiar sense of passing through rings of time. The newer

200
—

Knott's gave way to the seventies Knott's, which gave way to the Knott's of the sixties, fifties, and forties. I was time-traveling, not in an exotic Wellsian time machine, but with every footstep.

The deserted lobby of the Bird Cage looked as though time had stopped the day I left. On the walls were photos from various productions, some of which included me as resident goofball. On one wall were hall-of-fame eight-by-tens of graduates, including me, John Stuart, and Kathy Westmoreland. Stormie's photo was from the period: She was probably twenty when it was taken. It was hung at eye level, and I had the feeling of staring into her face, just as I did then.

I tugged on the theater door; it was locked. I was about to give up when I remembered a back entrance in the employees-only area, a clunky, oversize wooden gate that rarely locked because it was so rickety. I sneaked behind the theater and opened the door, which, for the millionth time, had failed to latch. The darkened theater flooded with sunlight, and I stepped inside and quickly shut the door. Light filtered in from the canvas roof, giving the Bird Cage a dim, golden hue. There I was, standing in a memory frozen in amber, and I experienced an over-whelming rush of sadness.

I went backstage and had a muscle memory of how to raise and lower the curtain, tying it off with a looping knot shown to me on my first day of work. I fiddled with the sole lighting rheostat, as antique as Edison. I stood on the stage and looked out at the empty theater and was overcome by the feeling of today being pressed into yesterday. I didn't realize how much this place had meant to me.

Driving home along the Santa Ana freeway, I was still unnerved. I asked myself what it was that had made this place capable of inducing in me such a powerful nostalgic shock. The answer floated clearly into my consciousness as though I had asked the question of a Magic 8-Ball: I wanted to be there again, if only for a day, indulging in high spirits and high jinks, before I turned professional, before comedy became serious.

I ALWAYS GAVE MY PERFORMANCES, even my five-minute talk show appearances, a beginning, a middle, and an end. It turned out that my stand-up career took that shape, too. I was in a conversation a few years ago with a friend, the painter Eric Fischl. We were comparing psychoanalysis with the making of art. I said, "Both require explorations of the subconscious, and in that way they are similar." He agreed, thought about it, then added, "But there is a fundamental difference between the two. In psychoanalysis, you try to retain a discovery; in art, once the thing is made, you let it go." He was right. I had not looked at or considered my stand-up career until writing this memoir; I had, in fact, abandoned it. Moving on and not looking back, not living in the past, was a way to trick myself into further creativity.

My career in stand-up gave me a vestigial sense of the crowd that I have relied upon over the last twenty-seven years. In the world of filmmaking, where there is no audience, where, in fact, quiet on the set is required, I sometimes try to determine if a particular idea is funny. I picture myself at the back of a darkened theater, watching the bit in question unspooling on the screen, and somewhere, in the black interior of my brain, I can hear the audience's response. Thankfully, when the movie is finally screened, I discover that my intuition is not always right. If it were, there would be no surprises left; I would be living in a dull comedy heaven.

I do not know if my act holds up these many years later. It is not for me to decide or even think about. Sometimes I hear or see a piece of the old show, and it sounds funny; sometimes I don't get it and can't figure out what all the fuss was about. I did, however, in the course of writing this memoir, come across routines and ad libs, long forgotten, that made me smile, like this description of a radio show in Austin, Texas, in the seventies, remembered by the host Sonny Melendrez:

"Steve Martin came directly from a recording session to debut his *Let's Get Small* album on my show. Before he left, he got very serious, and I truly thought we were seeing another side of him. He launched into a monologue of what seemed like sincere words of friendship. It took me by surprise, given the hour of silliness that had just taken place. 'Could this be the real Steve Martin?' I thought."

"Sonny, you know, I've listened to you for years, and I really feel like you've become my friend. I feel like I can ask you this question."

"Sure. Steve, you can ask me anything."

"What time is it?"

Acknowledgments

TWENTY YEARS AGO, I looked at the collected flotsam of my life and sent it off to an archivist, Candace Bothwell, who did an outstanding job of sequencing and preserving whatever she could. Later, I collected other cardboard boxes from my parents' house, some moldy from garage floods. Inside were sedimentary layers of collected junk, ephemera, snapshots, and yellowed newspaper clippings. Like a geologist, I was sometimes able to date items by their position in the stack. As much as I enjoyed the writing of this book, researching it was a new thrill for me. Finding a photo that confirmed a dim recollection of days gone by hooked me on the detective work, and the legwork—marching from my desk back and forth to the archival boxes—gave me something to do besides type, think, worry, and cry.

This book has allowed me to contact old friends and dig through their memories and memorabilia. All contacts have been pleasant and some quite moving. The arrival of a package of photos or copies of letters offered by a friend was like having an archaeological dig brought to my own home. People to whom I am grateful include, in no particular order, Gaylord Alexander, George and Carole McKelvey, John McClure, Nina Raggio, Gary Mule Deer, Dave Archer, John McEuen, Ivan Ultz, Dean Carter, Nick Pileggi, Kathy Westmoreland, Mitzi Trumbo, Melinda Dobbs, Stormie Omartian, Phil Carey, Bob Shayne, Betty Buckley (not the actress), Maple Byrne, and many others. They all helped fill in the past. In distilling my life, or a portion of my life, I may have left out people who had a crucial impact on me. Victoria Dailey deserves her own biography in order to tell the story of my debt to her, and Lorne Michaels deserves a bio, too, but he's already the subject of about ten.

Two valuable editors helped shape this book, Bill Phillips and Nan Graham, without whom I would still be wondering, "Where did I go wrong?" My representative, Esther Newberg, gave me tough love when she could have said, "You're beautiful, Stevie baby, you're beautiful." I also have to thank the host of friends I have used through the years as readers. I'm sure they're grateful that I have finally learned an important rule: You can't ask a friend to read your manuscript twice. I would string them out through the writing stages from clumsy first draft to shiny final, knowing I only had one shot at them, and, after the manuscript had improved, I always felt bad that a particular friend had read it when it stank. My thanks extend to Rebecca Wilson, Geoff Dyer, Nora Ephron, April Gornik, Eric Fischl, Adam Gopnik, Bruce McCall, Joan Stein, Ricky Jay, Mike Nichols, David Geffen, Pete Wernick, Anne Stringfield, and finally, the Internet: I have learned that people are uploading their lives into cyberspace and am convinced that one day all human knowledge and memory will exist on a suitable hard drive which, for preservation, will be flung out of the solar system to orbit a galaxy far, far away.

BORN STANDING UP

Photograph Credits

Photographs were provided courtesy of the author except for the following:

Page 6: © Morris Lafon

Pages 58 and 61: © Dean Carter

Page 69 and 94: © Mitzi Trumbo

Pages 77 and 82: © Nina Raggio

Page 93: © Cleo Trumbo

Pages 114 and 116: © Henry Diltz

Page 118: © William E. McEuen

Page 155: © Norman Seeff

Page 174: © 1978 Edie Baskin

Page 178: © John Malmquist/pixdude.com

Page 182: © Bill Thompson